The
Julia Language
Handbook
Julia v1.02

George Root

2019

The

Julia Language Handbook

George Root

Copyright © 2019 George Root

All Rights Reserved

January 2019

ISBN-13: 9781794681699

Table of Contents

Chapter 1

Introduction to Julia

I didn't want to write this book. I wanted to buy one like it. I actually did buy three of the Julia books that are available . All of them were less than helpful with inadequate explanations and with many examples that did not work. This was primarily because the version of Julia they were describing no longer exists. It has been superseded by Julia v1.0 and a lot of what they describe is no longer valid. Syntax has been changed and some functions have been eliminated. Other functions have been added. To get the book I wanted, I decided that I would have to write it.

I'm not a computer scientist nor a professional programmer. I'm an engineer with 25 years of experience writing complex system simulations using Fortran. I have recently become a fan of Python, but the idiocy of indexing arrays starting at 0 drives me crazy. Julia caught my attention because programming in Julia promised to be as easy as Python and arrays are indexed starting at 1. The result is this book that summarizes Julia programming and which contains examples that have all been tested to run under Julia v1.0. It is the book I wanted and I hope you find it useful as well.

Julia is the hot new programming language. It is the likely successor to Python as the preferred language for scientific and engineering applications. It is particularly suited to compute intensive tasks because it is a compiled language that runs nearly as fast as Fortran or C code. Some tests have found Julia to run roughly 30 times faster than Python. The Julia ecosystem consists of a "package" manager that permits including in your code, libraries of functions that support whatever task you may have.

Julia is a free, open source language that can be downloaded and installed on any modern computer. Complete instructions for doing this are included in Chapter 2.

Julia code can be run in a terminal app known as the **REPL** mode (**R**ead, **E**xecute, **P**rint, **L**oop Back and Repeat). This is very helpful for quickly checking your code syntax. The REPL mode has a help system accessed by typing shift-?. You can find information on any Julia function in this way.

In this book Julia examples executed in the REPL mode will look like this:

```
julia> a = [2;1;5]              # the Julia prompt
3-element Array{Int64,1}:
 2
 1
 5
```

Julia can also be run in the **Jupyter Notebook** environment just like Python. This makes code development as easy as with Python. Instructions for using both REPL and Notebook modes are included in Chapter 2.

1

Examples of code run in the Jupyter Notebook environment will look like this:

```
01   Angle  = collect(0.0:2.0:90.0)    # array of angles in degrees
02   Sine   = [sind(angle) for angle in Angle]
03   Cosine = [cosd(angle) for angle in Angle];
```

with line numbers to aid in explanations.

However, Julia is not without problems:

Julia is a "compiled" language. This means that the source code is converted into executable instructions the first time the code is run and those executable instructions are stored and re-executed on successive runs. This means that Julia code is very fast the **second** time it is run. The first time you run your code you have to wait for Julia to go out to the Git repository and download the latest versions of whatever code you need and then compile that code. This process can take time measured in minutes - not seconds. As a result code development is slower than with Python.

A second problem is that Julia is a work in progress. Improvements are constantly being crafted by small groups of volunteer programmers. Syntax changes occur so that code that ran yesterday may not run today. Because of this I have tested every code example used in this book and they all run - at least they do at the time this book is being written.

Another problem is that on-line documentation is, in many cases, obsolete describing Julia versions that no longer exist. The information in this book is current as of Julia v1.02. My primary purpose for writing this book has been to provide an up to date description of the Julia language and how to use it.

I hope that you find this book, and the Julia language itself, to be useful.

Chapter 2

Installing Julia

Installing Julia is a multi-step process. That is because there are two different ways in which to use Julia and they both should be installed.

Julia can be run as if it were an interpreted language in a terminal window. Type a Julia statement and see the results immediately in the terminal. This environment is referred to as the "REPL" -- Read, Execute, Print, Loop.

```
● ● ●                    🏠 GRRoot — julia — 98×75
Last login: Thu Oct 25 13:41:04 on ttys000
Temps-iMac:~ GRRoot$ exec '/Applications/Julia-1.0.app/Contents/Resources/julia/bin/julia'
        _
   _       _ _(_)_     |  Documentation: https://docs.julialang.org
  (_)     | (_) (_)    |
   _ _   _| |_  __ _   |  Type "?" for help, "]?" for Pkg help.
  | | | | | | |/ _` |  |
  | | |_| | | | (_| |  |  Version 1.0.1 (2018-09-29)
 _/ |\__'_|_|_|\__'_|  |  Official https://julialang.org/ release
|__/                   |

julia> x = 5
5

julia> y = 10
10

julia> x+y
15
```

Julia can also be run in a "Jupyter Notebook" environment. This environment is much more suited to writing code to be compiled and run after editing.

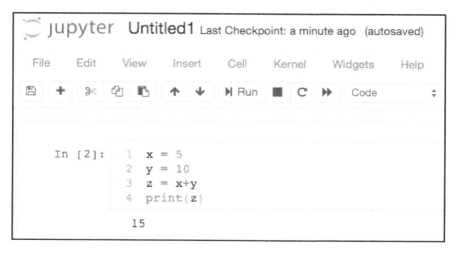

The best way to install the Jupyter Notebook environment is to install the "Anaconda" package. This package includes Jupyter Notebook and the Python programming language. Plotting in Julia is most easily done using the Python "PyPlot" package. The interface between Julia and Python is accomplished by an app package named "IJulia" which will also be installed.

2.1 - Installing the Anaconda/Python Package

The first step is to download and install the Anaconda package from the Anaconda website at www.anaconda.com/download :

There are versions for Windows, macOS, and Linux. All of the examples illustrated in this book use the macOS version. Choose the version you prefer and that will take you to the download window:

This web page also provides access to a lot of documentation for Anaconda as well as Python:

You will be asked where to install the Anaconda package. The default is to install it in your home folder.

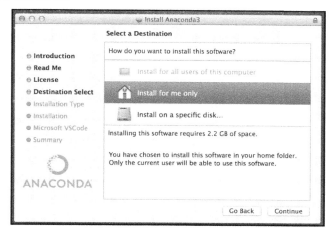

As part of the Anaconda installation you will be given the option to add the Microsoft Visual Studio Code environment to your installation.

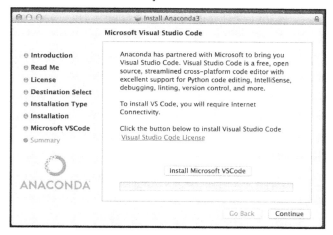

Once the Anaconda installation is complete, you are ready to run a Jupyter Notebook. A Jupyter Notebook is actually an HTML app that runs in your default browser. To launch a Jupyter Notebook you have to first open a Terminal window and type Jupyter Notebook.

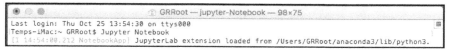

That will open your default web browser and display a Jupyter Notebook as illustrated on the next page. If your default browser is not Chrome, you might want to switch to Chrome for running Jupyter Notebooks. Some other browsers have issues with Jupyter.

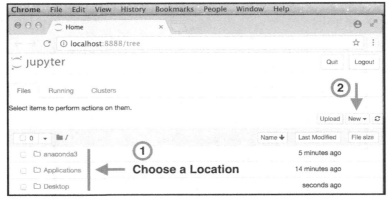

To create a new Notebook, you will first choose a location for the Notebook as illustrated at "1" in the figure. Then click on the "New" button shown at "2" in the figure.

At this point, Julia has not been installed so Python is the only type of Notebook available.

If you are not familiar with computer programming, you might find it easier to learn using Python. There are a host of introductory books that will help you learn. Julia is a relatively new language and it is evolving fairly rapidly. Many of the books and websites covering Julia are out of date and many of the examples no longer work.

2.2 - Installing Julia

Julia is an app and it can be downloaded and installed as any other app. Start at the julialang.org/downloads/ page in your browser:

Once again you can download Julia versions for Windows, macOS and Linux. Unless you intend to join the development of the Julia language, download the latest "stable" version.

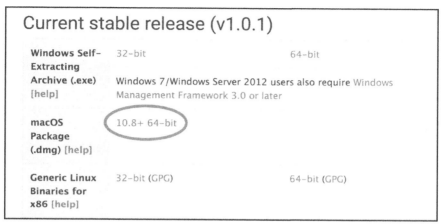

Current stable release (v1.0.1)

Windows Self-Extracting Archive (.exe) [help]	32–bit	64–bit
	Windows 7/Windows Server 2012 users also require Windows Management Framework 3.0 or later	
macOS Package (.dmg) [help]	10.8+ 64–bit	
Generic Linux Binaries for x86 [help]	32–bit (GPG)	64–bit (GPG)

For macOS what you download is a disk image (.dmg) file. Double click on the dmg file and a "disk" will open with the Julia app inside. Simply drag the Julia app icon

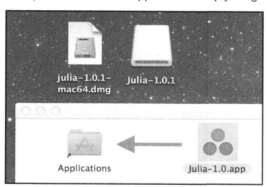

onto the Applications folder as illustrated above. You can now treat Julia as any other app. Double clicking on the Julia app icon will launch the Terminal app and start the Julia REPL with the cursor waiting for your first input.

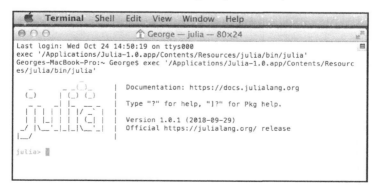

But before you type anything we need to install the IJulia package that will link Julia with the Jupyter Notebook system and with the plotting capabilities of Python.

2.3 - Installing IJulia

The basic Julia installation includes many capabilities, but there are dozens, perhaps hundreds of other "packages" that can be added to the base Julia installation to add functionality not built into Julia itself. IJulia is one of those packages. Packages are added to Julia using the Package Manager (pkg). Start by typing a right-square-bracket ( ]) at the julia prompt:

```
julia> ]                          # this launches the pkg manager
(v1.0) pkg> add IJulia            # type add IJulia
    .
    .                             # a long installation process
    .

delete                            # press the delete key
julia>                            # returns you to the julia prompt
```

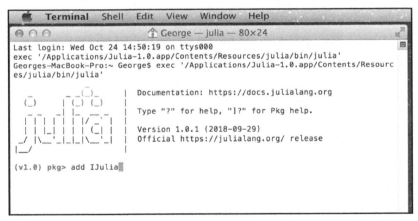

When you use the pkg manager to add IJulia, or any package for that matter, Julia goes out to the github repository and downloads the package. It then compiles that package, so this whole process may take several minutes depending upon Internet traffic.

You will never use IJulia directly. IJulia provides the linkages necessary to allow you to run Julia in a Jupyter Notebook. It also provides the linkages that allow you to use some Python functionality -- specifically the Python plotting capability.

2.4 - Using Julia in a Jupyter Notebook

To start the Jupyter Notebook environment, open a Terminal window and type Jupyter Notebook:

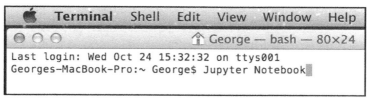

When you hit Return or Enter, your default web browser will launch with the Jupyter Notebook running in a browser window:

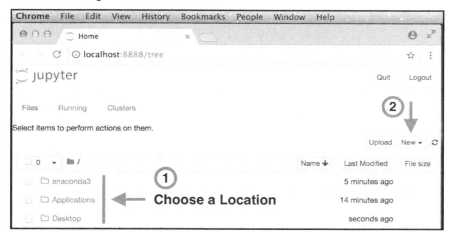

As described previously, to create a new Julia Notebook, you first choose a location at "1" in this figure. You can open any of the folders shown to drill down to the folder where you want your code to reside. If you need to do a lot of folder manipulation at this point, you might prefer to do that before launching the Jupyter Notebook app.

The next step in creating a Julia program is to open a "New" document as illustrated at "2" in the figure. If everything has gone properly up to this point, you should now see options to create a new Python program or a new Julia program. Choose Julia and you will get a Jupyter Notebook with Julia running:

By default your code is named "Untitled". You can give your code a more meaningful name by clicking on the current name and entering a new name. In the illustration below, I have named this code "JuliaNoteBookTest01". In your machine's file system your code will show up with the name "Name.**ipynb**". Unfortunately you cannot launch the Jupyter Notebook by double clicking on this file name. You have to open a Terminal window and go through the steps already outlined.

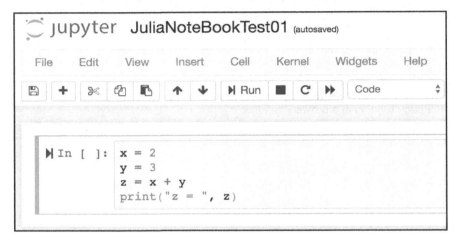

When you type into a Notebook cell, you are in editing mode. This is indicated by a green outline around the cell which you cannot see in this black & white image. When you type, Jupyter autosaves your code every few seconds.

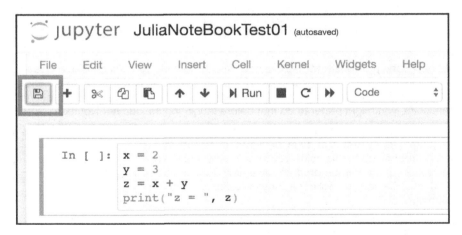

When you are finished editing your code, you do two things to give it a test run:

The first is to click on the "floppy disk" icon shown outlined in this figure. This will save your code and switch from editing mode to execution mode. This will be indicated by the cell outline turning blue.

To actually run your code, click on the "Run" icon shown outlined in the figure on the next page.

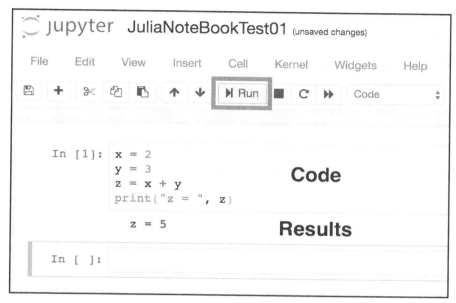

You can also execute your code by typing shift-enter in the editing window.

Execution of your code may take longer than you might expect. This is because Julia is a compiled language and as such, it must be compiled before it runs. This compilation process may take more or less time depending upon your code. Ironically, code written in Python often executes faster than code written in Julia for this reason. Of course, once the Julia code has been compiled, it can be run again without re-compilation and in that case it will run much faster than Python code. Some tests have shown it might run 10-30 times faster.

When your code runs, the results are displayed in the space below the cell containing your code. For example, the "z = 5" result illustrated above. This includes any plots your code produces.

You can execute shell commands from the Jupyter Notebook by executing a statement like this. You can use any shell command instead of `pwd`.

```
In [1]:    1 run(`pwd`)

          /Users/GRRoot/Documents/Book-Julia/SampleCode
```

Note the backtick characters (`) they are not apostrophes.

To end your Notebook session, go back to the Terminal you used to launch the Notebook and type control-c and then confirm by typing "y". Or, you can just type control-c twice. That terminates the Notebook, but it leaves you still in the Terminal app. You can quit that as you usually quit an app - cmd-Q on macOS.

That should be enough to get you started. There is a lot more to learn about the Jupyter Notebook environment and I encourage you to do some research. This is a good place to start:

https://jupyter.readthedocs.io/en/latest/running.html#running

The Jupyter Notebook has an extensive Help function at the right end of the Note Book menu. Three items that you might find useful are:

1. User Interface Tour
2. Keyboard Shortcuts
3. MatPlotLib Reference

We will be using the Python MatPlotLib package to do plotting in Julia later so this would be a good place to find out about its capabilities.

"TAB Completion" works in the Notebook environment. For example, type pri and hit TAB. The function name "print" will be completed.

TAB completion also works to insert Greek characters. For example: type \alpha and hit TAB:

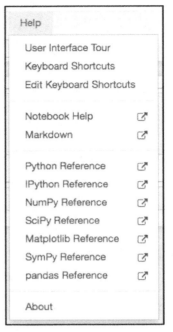

2.5 - Using the REPL

There are a few tricks to make the REPL more useful.

- When you type an expression at the Julia prompt, the REPL evaluates it as soon as you type return and displays the results on the next line:

  julia> 42
  42

- If you type a semicolon after the expression, it will suppress displaying the result:

  julia> 42;

- The last result from evaluating a Julia expression in the REPL is stored in a variable named "ans". You can print "ans" or use it in further computations:

  julia> ans
  42

  julia> ans+3
  45

- You can use the up/down keys to scroll up and down through the previously entered REPL statements - even those entered in a previous REPL session. This is particularly useful if you type something and it generates an error. If you type the up key, that will scroll up to the last statement where you can edit that statement and try again.

- You cannot use the mouse cursor to move around in the REPL. You must use the cursor keys (up/down right/left).

- If you type a semicolon at the Julia prompt, you will be switched to shell mode where you can execute any shell command supported by your OS:

```
julia> ;                                    # type a semicolon to switch to shell mode
shell> pwd                                  # pwd displays the current working directory
/Users/GRRoot

julia> ;                                    # you must type a semicolon each time
shell> ls                                   # ls lists the contents of the current directory
Applications
Documents
Downloads
...

julia> ;                                              # you must type a semicolon
shell> cd /Users/GRRoot/Documents/   # cd changes the current directory
/Users/GRRoot/Documents

julia> ;                                    # you must type a semicolon
shell> pwd                                  # pwd displays the current directory
/Users/GRRoot/Documents/           # the current directory = Documents
```

- REPL provides "TAB Completion". Start typing and after a few letters hit TAB - you may have to hit TAB twice. That will list everythig REPL knows that starts with the letters you typed.

```
julia> so                                   # I typed TAB after the 'o'
something                                   # the list of Julia names starting with so
sort
sort!
sortperm
sortperm!
sortslices
```

- Julia has a large built-in help system. To get help on any Julia topic, type a question mark (?) followed by what you need help on:

```
julia> ?
help?> print
```

Julia help will search for entries that match what you have typed and will produce a list of related matches. So, for example, typing "print" will result in this list of possibilities:

- print
- println
- printstyled
- sprint
- isprint

- prevind
- parentindices
- precision

You can invoke "help" on each of these print related functions to see what they do.

The REPL returns to the Julia prompt after each call to "help". Here is an edited example of "help" for the print command:

print([io::IO], xs...)   # [io::IO] means that parameter io is of Type IO

Write to io (or to stdout if io is not given) a text representation of values xs. The representation used by print includes minimal formatting and tries to avoid Julia specific details. Printing nothing, print(), prints a blank line.

Examples:

```
julia> print("Hello World!")
Hello World!

julia> x = 10;
julia> print("x = ", x)        # prints a string and then the value of x
x = 10

julia> print("x = $x")         # the value of x can be inserted into the string
x = 10                         # using the syntax $x inside the string
```

Help is a good way to determine whether or not a given function exists. For example, there used to be a Julia function "linspace" that mimicked the Python function.

```
help?> linspace
Couldn't find linspace. Perhaps you meant isspace or instances
```

Alas, linspace no longer exists. It has been replaced with range():

```
help?> range
```

range(start; length, stop, step=1)

Given a starting value, construct a range either by length or from start to stop, optionally with a given step (defaults to 1, a UnitRange). Either length or stop is required. If length, stop, and step are all specified, they must agree.

If length and stop are provided and step is not, the step size will be computed automatically such that there are length linearly spaced elements in the range (a LinRange).

If step and stop are provided and length is not, the overall range length will be computed automatically such that the elements are step spaced (a StepRange).

```
julia> range(1, length=100)    #step=1 is the default if none is supplied
1:100
julia> range(1, stop=100)      #step=1 is the default if none is supplied
1:100
julia> range(1, step=5, length=100)
1:5:496
julia> range(1, step=5, stop=100)
1:5:96
```

Chapter 3

Julia Style Conventions

Before we get to actually writing Julia programs, it will be useful to review some Julia conventions.

The basic code type is a function.

Write functions, not just scripts

Writing code as a series of steps at the top level is a quick way to get started solving a problem, but you should try to divide a program into functions as soon as possible. Functions are more reusable and testable, and clarify what steps are being done and what their inputs and outputs are. Furthermore, code inside functions tends to run much faster than top level code, due to how Julia's compiler works.

It is also worth emphasizing that functions should take arguments, instead of operating directly on global variables

Package = GitHub syntax combination of metadata and module

Module = collection of related functions

Function = collection of related Methods

3.1 - Julia Naming Conventions

Julia does not enforce strict rules about how you can name items, but there are a few style guidelines that might be good to know before you start typing. These are the guidelines followed by Julia itself and so if you also use them, that will give your code a more unified style.

Variable Names

- Variable names are case sensitive.
- Variable names begin with a letter or underscore character or a subset of Unicode characters
- Subsequent characters can be numbers, or underscore
- Variable names can contain, or be, Unicode symbols
- Variable names cannot be built-in key words

Function and Macro Names

- Function and macro names are all lowercase. If the name consists of multiple words, no separation between words is used. If necessary for readability, use underscores as word separators.

- Names of functions that modify their arguments end with !

Type and Module Names

- Module and Type names begin with a capital letter and use camel case thereafter: Float64, Int16.

3.2 - Macros vs Functions

If you have a task that could be written as either a macro or as a function, choose the function. Functions run faster than macros.

Chapter 4

Julia Data Types

Julia variables are strongly typed. You can define the variable's type explicitly or Julia will deduce the variable's type by its use in the program.

```
julia> x=1; typeof(x)          # "1" is an integer => Int64
Int64

julia> x=1.0; typeof(x)        # "1.0" is a floating point number
Float64

julia> x="A String"; typeof(x)
String

julia> x="C"; typeof(x)        # notice the double quotes => string
String

julia> x='C'; typeof(x)        # notice the single quotes => character
Char
```

Variable names may consist of upper and lower case letters, numbers and the underscore (_) character. Variable names are case sensitive x≠X. The exclamation point (!) is also used but its use is limited to the names of functions that modify their input argument values.

Underscore characters can also be used in numbers to make reading them easier:

```
julia> x = 1_000_000          # x is an Int64
1000000

julia> x = 1_000_000.0        # x is a Float64
1.0e6
```

There are conventions for naming variables:

- Variable names can begin with a lowercase letter or an underscore character.
- Variable names are generally all lower case with underscore characters used to separate words in the name.
- The first character in the names of types and modules is uppercase as illustrated above. Word separation is done using camel case.
- Names of functions and macros are all lowercase. Names of functions that modify the values of their input arguments end with an exclamation point (!).

These conventions are not mandatory.

As in all programming languages, there are reserved keywords that may not be used as variable names: for, if, else, end, while, and so forth. If you try to define one of these reserved keywords, Julia will slap your wrist:

```
julia> for = 1
ERROR: syntax: unexpected "="
```

4.1 - Math Constants:

Julia provides a set of built-in math constants. One of these is named "pi" and that name cannot be redefined.

> julia> **pi**
> π = 3.1415926535897…
>
> julia> pi = 4
> ERROR: cannot assign variable MathConstants.pi

Notice that Julia has replaced the name "pi" with the single character name π which can be typed on a Macintosh keyboard as option-p. In your code you can use either "pi" or "π".

Julia provides other math constants, but they are harder to get to. The name of the constant must be prefixed with "Base.MathConstants.". So, for example, the value of "e" = the base of natural logarithms can be obtained by:

> julia> Base.MathConstants.**e**
> e = 2.7182818284590…

But that value for "e" does not persist:

> julia> e
> ERROR: UndefVarError: e not defined

In order to define the variable "e" to be equal to the constant "e" you have to do it explicitly:

> julia> e = Base.MathConstants.**e**
> e = 2.7182818284590…

That value will now persist, but it is a variable and not a constant:

> julia> e
> e = 2.7182818284590…
>
> julia> e = 4   # the value assigned to "e" can be changed
> 4

The values for other math constants can be found by using:

> julia> Base.MathConstants.**catalan**
> catalan = 0.9159655941772…
>
> julia> Base.MathConstants.**eulergamma**
> γ = 0.5772156649015…
>
> julia> Base.MathConstants.**golden**
> φ = 1.6180339887498…

4.2 - Integer Variables

Julia integers can be of types: Int8, Int16, Int32, Int64, and Int128 where the binary numbers indicate the bit length of the computer representation of the integer number. If no bit length is specified, it defaults to the word length of the computer being used - generally 64 bits on modern computers. The integer bit length can be specified as follows:

```
julia> x = Int16(100); typeof(x)
Int16
```

There are also unsigned integers with the same bit lengths, **UInt64** for example.

The largest and smallest representable integers for each integer type can be found using the **typemax** and **typemin** functions:

```
julia> typemax(Int64)
9223372036854775807

julia> typemin(Int64)
-9223372036854775808
```

Julia implements "bignum" or arbitrary precision arithmetic:

```
julia> x = big(1); typeof(x)
BigInt
```

Further discussion of bignum arithmetic is beyond the scope of this book.

It is worth noting that the result of integer arithmetic may not be integer:

```
julia> x=5
julia> y=2
julia> x/y     # the " / " operator implies floating point division
2.5

julia> x÷y     # the " ÷ " ( option-/ ) operator implies integer division
2
```

Integer division can also be performed using the functions **div** and **rem**:

```
julia> div(x,y)        # integer division x÷y
2

julia> rem(x,y)        # the remainder after integer division x÷y
1
```

If you frequently use the Type declarations Int64 or UInt64, Julia allows you to use the aliases Int and UInt for the system default Integer and Unsigned Integer Types:

```
julia> x = Int(45.0)
julia> typeof(x)
Int64

julia> Int == Int64
true

julia> UInt == UInt64
true
```

Unsigned Integers are input and output as hexadecimal values:

```
julia> y = UInt(45.0)
0x000000000000002d
```

4.3 - Floating Point Variables

There are several ways to define a floating point variable:

Use a decimal point in the number representation:

```
julia> x = 1.0; typeof(x)      # use a decimal point
Float64
```

Use exponential notation:

```
julia> x = 1e8; typeof(x)      # exponent " e " => Float64
Float64

julia> x = 1f8; typeof(x)      # exponent " f " => Float32
Float32
```

Notice that using exponential notation with an "e" yields a Float64 number, sometimes called "double precision". But using exponential notation with an "f" yields a Float32 number - sometimes called "single precision". Note that for exponential notation, e==E but f≠F:

```
julia> x = 3.2f8
3.2f8

julia> x = 3.2F8              # must use lower case f
ERROR: UndefVarError: F8 not defined
```

You can also explicitly define the data type:

```
julia> x = Float64(1); typeof(x)
Float64

julia> x = Float32(1.0); typeof(x)
Float32
```

You can convert between Float32 and Float64 or visa versa:

```
julia> x = 5.0f6; typeof(x)
Float32

julia> y = Float64(x); typeof(y)
Float64
```

The "typemin" and "typemax" functions are not particularly informative for floating point numbers:

```
julia> typemax(Float64)
Inf

julia> typemin(Float64)
-Inf
```

Notice that "inf" (infinity) is a floating point number that is greater than the largest or smaller than the smallest number that can be expressed by the machine representation of a floating point number. Infinity can be returned by some floating point mathematical operations:

```
julia> 1/0
Inf

julia> -1/0
-Inf
```

"Inf" can be used in logical (Boolean) tests:

```
julia> x = 10; x<Inf
true
```

"Inf" can be used to find the max and min numbers that can be expressed by a Float64 variable:

```
julia> prevfloat(Inf)   # the previous floating point number less than Inf
1.7976931348623157e308
```

This is the largest Float64 number that can be expressed by the machine implementation.

Similarly:

```
julia> nextfloat(0.0)   # the next floating point number greater than 0
5.0e-324
```

This is the smallest Float64 number expressible.

The function **eps(n)** returns the increment between floating point number **n** and the next representable floating point number:

```
julia> eps(1.0)
2.220446049250313e-16

julia> eps(100.0)
1.4210854715202004e-14
```

"**NaN**" ("Not a Number") is also a mathematical value that can be used in Boolean tests:

```
julia> x=10; x == NaN       # is x a NaN?
false

julia> 0/0
NaN
```

4.4 - Boolean Variables

Boolean variables are of type **Bool** and can have only one of two possible constant values: "**true**" or "**false**". Variables can be assigned to be true or false using simple equality:

```
julia> b = true
true

julia> c = false
false

julia> d = false; typeof(d)
Bool
```

Boolean variables are used in logical tests.

```
julia> b == c           # is b equal to c?
false
```

As in many programming languages, true = 1 and false = 0.

```
julia> a = 1; a == true
true

julia> a = 0; a == false
true
```

Any other numerical value is neither true nor false

```
julia> a = 10; a == true
false

julia> a = 10; a == false
false
```

Boolean tests for equality, inequality and so forth are accomplished by these symbols:

- equality ==
- inequality != or ≠ (option = on the Mac keyboard)
- less than <
- less than or equal to <= or ≤ (option < on the Mac keyboard)
- greater than >
- greater than or equal to >= or ≥ (option > on the Mac keyboard)
- identical to ===

Here are some simple examples:

```
julia> 2 == 2
true

julia> 2 > 3
false

julia> 2 != 3
true

julia> 2.0 == 2
true

julia> 2.0 === 2
false
```

Notice the difference between the last two tests. "==" tests whether the two values are numerically equal while "===" tests whether the two values are identical to each other. A floating point number is not identical to an integer even though they may both represent the same number.

Just as a side note, these tests do not work on NaNs:

```
julia> NaN == NaN
false

julia> NaN != NaN
true
```

Julia supports the negation operator !:

```
julia> x = true          # variable X is assigned to be "true"
true

julia> !x                # !x (not x) is "false"
false
```

4.5 - Missing Variables

Real world data often has some data items that are missing or are obviously wrong. Julia DataFrames, which we will discuss later, has the ability to mark these data items and to ignore them when computing parameters such as mean and standard deviation.

To mark missing data items, Julia has a special data Type "Missing". The Type Missing has only one instance, missing. DataFrame computations simply ignore any data items that are marked by the symbol missing.

4.6 - Characters

Julia represents a character as a 32 bit object so Julia can handle ASCII and UTF-8 symbols. ASCII characters are the "standard" letters and numbers plus a few control characters such as carriage return and line feed that were found on typewriters and teletype machines way back in the dark ages.

UTF-8 symbols include all of the ASCII characters in addition to many needed to express foreign languages. In particular some Greek symbols used in math such as pi are UTF-8 characters and are not found in the ASCII set.

Julia uses "C" syntax to represent the ASCII control characters that do not appear on a computer keyboard. The "C" syntax uses the back-slash character (\ ) to "escape" the normal flow of characters and to insert a control character. The most useful of these control characters are:

- **\n** is newline
- **\t** is horizontal tab
- **** types a single backslash
- **\'** types a single quotation mark
- **\"** types a double quotation mark

The newline control character (\n) is often used in Julia print functions to end one line of characters and to start a newline at the left margin. Newline is a combination of carriage return and linefeed. "Newline" and "Line Feed" are not the same but are frequently used as if they were.

Here is an example of two print statement without newline characters:

```
julia> print("This is the 1st line."); print("This is the 2nd line.")
This is the 1st line. This is the 2nd line.
```

Both print statements got printed on the same line. By inserting a newline (\n) character in the first print statement, the second print statement gets printed on a new line.

```
julia> print("This is the 1st line.\n"); print("This is the 2nd line.")
This is the 1st line.
This is the 2nd line.
```

Julia implements a **println** statement that automatically inserts a newline character at the end of the printed text.

> julia> **println**("This is the 1st line."); **println**("This is the 2nd line.")
> This is the 1st line.
> This is the 2nd line.

If you end a println statement with a newline character, you will get double spacing:

> julia> **println**("This is the 1st line.\n"); **println**("This is the 2nd line.")
> This is the 1st line.
>
> This is the 2nd line.

Defining Characters:

In Julia a single character surrounded with single quotes is of type Char:

> julia> a = 'C'; typeof(a)
> Char

A single character surrounded by double quotes, is a String containing only a single character:

> julia> b = "C"; typeof(b)
> String

A single character surrounded by triple quotes is a String containing only a single character.

> julia> c = """"C"""; typeof(c)
> String

This construct would be used if the string will contain quotation marks:

> julia> println("""This is 'quoted' text""")
> This is 'quoted' text

Character Arrays:

Character arrays can be defined using the character array type definition:

> julia> c = Char[]
> 0-element Array{Char,1}

The character array "c" can then be filled by "pushing" characters onto the end of the array:

> julia> c = Char[]; **push!**(c,'H')
> 1-element Array{Char,1}:
> 'H'

Pushing another character onto the array does not result in a String, but rather an array of single characters:

> julia> c = Char[]; **push!**(c,'H'); **push!**(c,'i')
> 2-element Array{Char,1}:
> 'H'
> 'i'

Non-ASCII Characters:

Sometime it is convenient to be able to use non-ASCII characters in your code. For example, Julia has a built-in constant named "pi":

```
julia> pi
π = 3.1415926535897...
```

Notice that Julia converts "pi" to the standard single character symbol for that constant π:

```
julia> π
π = 3.1415926535897...
```

You can use non-ASCII characters in your Julia code if you think that will make the code easier to read and understand. On a Macintosh keyboard, many non-ASCII characters can be typed by holding down the "option" key and typing one of the keys on the keyboard. For example, typing "option-p" results in π.

There are several "option keys" that define standard math symbols that might be useful in your code. On a Macintosh keyboard these option key combinations are:

option-p π	option-o ø	option-w ∑	option-m μ
option-< ≤	option-> ≥	option-/ ÷	option-z Ω
option-5 ∞	option-= ≠	option-d ∂	option-j Δ
option-x ≈	option-v √	shift-option-= ±	

Some other non-ASCII characters that might be useful:

shift-option-2 €	shift-option-8 °	option-2 ™	option-3 £
option-4 ¢	option-g ©	option-y ¥	

You can use these non-ASCII characters just as if they were ASCII characters:

```
julia> Δ = 3.5
3.5
```

You can also type non-ASCII characters in the REPL using LaTeX syntax. For example typing \beta and hitting TAB results in:

```
julia> \beta          # hit TAB rather than Return
julia> β
```

4.6 - Strings

Strings can be defined by enclosing a list of characters inside double (or triple) quotes:

> julia> s = "Hello World"; typeof(s)
> String

> julia> s
> "Hello World"

The contents of the string array can be indexed as with other array types. To extract a single character from the string:

> julia> s = "Hello World"
> julia> s[7]   # remember that Julia arrays are indexed from 1 to N
> 'W'

To extract a range of characters from the string:

> julia> s[1:5]   # remember that Julia arrays are indexed from 1 to N
> "Hello"

However, shortcuts that are permitted in Python do not work as expected in Julia:

> julia> s[:5]
> 'o'

In Python, this would have yielded "Hello ". In Julia it yields the single character at index "5" which is the letter "o" in this case. Thus expressions like s[:5] should never be used in Julia. Write s[5] instead to avoid confusion.

The following expression, which in Python would have yielded the string "llo World" yields an error in Julia.

> julia> s[2:]
> ERROR: syntax: missing last argument in "2:" range expression

Arrays in Julia are indexed using a "range" notation consisting of three integer numbers start:step:end. start and end are mandatory. "step" defaults to "1" if not specified:

> julia> s[1:5]
> "Hello"

> julia> s[1:2:5]
> "Hlo"

Strings can be indexed backward if desired by using a negative step value:

> julia> s[5:-1:1]
> "olleH"

Using the range notation to extract a portion of a string actually makes a copy of that portion of the string.

> julia> s[2:4]
> "ell"

There is also a SubString function that does not make a copy:

> julia> SubString(s,2,4)
> "ell"

Julia allows the word "**end**" to be used as an index into a string:

```
julia> s = "Hello World"

julia> s[end]
'd'

julia> s[end-4]
'W')
```

And remember that Julia strings are not indexed as are Python and C strings!

```
julia> s[0]
ERROR: BoundsError: attempt to access "Hello World" at index [0]
```

Also note that s[index] is not the same as s[index:index]. The first returns a character and the second returns a string containing a single character.

```
julia> s = "Hello World"
julia> s[7]
'W'                    # note the single quotes => Character

julia> s[7:7]
"W"                    # note the double quotes => String
```

Strings, once defined, are immutable. The contents of the string array cannot be changed. Attempting to change an element of the string will result in an error:

```
julia> s = "Hello World"
julia> s[7] = 'M'
ERROR: MethodError
```

Strings can be concatenated using the multiplication operator *:

```
julia> a = "Hello "     # note the space after Hello
julia> b = "World"
julia> c = a * b        # if you are not familiar with Julia, this is confusing
"Hello World"
```

Strings can also be concatenated using the $ operator which might be less confusing than using the multiplication operator:

```
julia> "$a$b"
"Hello World"
```

The $ operator can also be used to insert variable values into strings:

```
julia> age=21; s = "I wish I were $age again"
"I wish I were 21 again"
```

Strings can be decomposed by a function named "split":

```
julia> s = "Bob Jim Joe"        # a string of strings separated by spaces
julia> a = split(s)        # by default split splits the string on white space
3-element Array{SubString{String},1}:   # the result is an array of strings
"Bob"
"Jim"
"Joe"

julia> a[2]             # this array of strings can be indexed just as any array
"Jim"


julia> a[2]= "John"     # elements of the string array can be redefined
"John"
```

27

```
julia> a
"Bob"
"John"                    # a[2] has been redefined
"Joe"

julia> s                  # the original array s has not been changed
"Bob Jim Joe"

julia> b = "Tom,Tim,Tony"  # a string of strings separated by commas
julia> c = split(b,',')    # split b on commas
"Tom"
"Tim"
"Tony"

julia> d = c[1]*c[2]*c[3]   # the string can be concatenated using *
"TomTimTony"

julia> c[2] = "John"       # c[2] is redefined from "Tim" to "John"

julia> d = c[1]*','*c[2]*','*c[3]   # the string d has been redefined
"Tom,John,Tony"
```

4.7 - Structures

Structures are composite data types. A composite type is a collection of named elements. An instance of a composite structure can be treated as a single value.

Structures are defined using the following syntax:

```
julia> struct Member
           name::String
           age::Int64
           weight::Float64
       end
```

This defines a data structure named "Member" with fields named "name", "age", and "weight". Instances of this composite data Type named m1 can be created using this syntax:

```
julia> m1 = Member("Joe",25,175)
Member("Joe", 25, 175.0)
```

Another instance named m2 is created in the same way.

```
julia> m2 = Member("Jim",50,225)
Member("Jim", 50, 225.0)
```

Individual elements of the Member data structure can be recovered using the "dot" syntax:

```
julia> m1.name
"Joe"

julia> typeof(m1)        # confirmation that m1 is of Type "Member"
Member
```

A list of the field names of a data structure can be found using the "fieldnames" function:

> julia> **fieldnames**(Member)
>
> (:name, :age, :weight)

Composite objects declared with struct are immutable; they cannot be modified after construction. A structure can contain mutable objects, such as arrays. Those container objects will remain mutable. Only the fields of the structure object itself cannot be changed to point to different objects. See "Mutable vs Immutable" in the Functions chapter.

If you try to redefine the value attached to a structure field, you will raise an error:

> julia> m2.weight = 245.0
>
> **ERROR**: type Member is immutable

It is possible to define a mutable structure as follows:

> julia> **mutable struct** MMember   # note the "mutable" keyword
>   name::String
>   age::Int64
>   weight::Float64
>   end

> julia> mm1 = MMember("Joe",25,175)
> MMember("Joe", 25, 175.0)   # mm1.name = Joe

> julia> mm1.name = "Frank"   # a new value can be assigned to fields
> "Frank"

Chapter 5

Functions

In the previous chapter we introduced various types of data. In this chapter we will discuss combining these data variables into useful results using Julia programs. Complex functions are written by combining simple arithmetic operations and other mathematical functions. Julia provides dozens of these elementary operators and functions. The following sections will discuss some of these.

For additional information on Julia provided mathematical functions and everything related to Julia refer to:

https://docs.julialang.org

5.1 - Arithmetic Operators

This table lists some of the simple arithmetic operations that Julia uses to build complex functions:

Julia Arithmetic Operators	
x + y	add x and y
x - y	subtract y from x
x * y	multiply x and y
x / y	floating point divide x by y
x ÷ y	integer divide x by y
x % y	remainder after integer division
x ^ y	x to the y power

Julia allows the multiplication symbol, *, to be omitted in cases where there is no ambiguity. For example:

```
julia> x = 2.5
julia> y = 2*x        # including the ' * ' symbol is unambiguous
5.0

julia> y = 2x         # omitting the ' * ' symbol is also unambiguous
5.0
```

31

However, if you choose to omit the multiplication symbol, * , then some expressions that might seem OK to you may be rejected by Julia.

```
julia> x=5           # assign a value to the variable x
julia> (x-1)x        # implicit multiplication works
20

julia> x(x-1)        # but this doesn't work
ERROR: MethodError: objects of type Int64 are not callable
```

The problem is that Julia has interpreted the string "x(" as the start of a function definition.

```
julia> (x-1)(x+1)    # this doesn't work either
ERROR: MethodError: objects of type Int64 are not callable

julia> (x-1)*(x+1)   # this does work
24
```

In many cases parentheses are optional, but be sure you know how Julia will interpret the expression without parentheses.

$2\char`^3x = 2\char`^(3x)$ not $(2\char`^3)*x$

$2x\char`^3 = 2*(x\char`^3)$ not $(2x)\char`^3$

Here's another possible surprise:

```
julia> s1 = "string1 "; s2 = "string2"
julia> s1*s2                            # * applied to strings = concatenate
"string1 string2"
```

So, if you choose to save a few characters typing you may be spending a lot of time debugging your code.

5.2 - Math Functions

Julia provides all of the common mathematical functions.

Many of these math functions have alternate, more complex, versions. For example, the round() function allows you to set the rounding direction: up or down. For more information on all of these functions, or to search for a function that is not listed here, please refer to the website shown above or, at the Julia prompt, type ?name where "name" is the name of the item you want help on.

Math Functions	
hypot(x,y)	computes sqrt(x^2 + y^2)
hypot(xArray)	computes sqrt(sumof(x[i]^2)) for all i
log(x)	natural logarithm of x
log2(x)	logarithm of x to base 2
log10(x)	logarithm of x to base 10
log(base,x)	logarithm of x to base b. If b=2 or 10 use log2 or log10
log1p(x)	logarithm of (1 + x)
exp(x)	e^x
exp2(x)	2^x
exp10(x)	10^x
expm1(x)	e^x - 1
modf(x)	returns a tuple (fractional part, integral part) of x
round(x)	rounds x to the nearest integer
round(x; digits=n)	rounds x keeping n digits after the decimal point
ceil(x)	returns nearest integral value ≥ x
floor(x)	returns nearest integral value ≤ x
trunc(x)	returns nearest integral value whose abs value ≤ x
min(a, b, c, ...)	returns the minimum of the arguments
max(a, b, c, ...)	returns the maximum of the arguments
minimum(array)	returns the minimum value in the array
maximum(array)	returns the maximum value in the array
abs(x)	absolute value of x
abs2(x)	abs(x)^2
sqrt(x)	returns square root of x
cbrt(x)	returns cube root of x
factorial(n::Integer)	factorial of n; n must be integer
gcd(a,b)	greatest common positive divisor

5.3 - Trig Functions

Julia provides all of the standard trigonometric functions "out of the box".

Trig Functions	
sin(a), cos(a), tan(a)	sine, cosine and tangent of (a) in **radians**
sind(a), cosd(a), tand(a)	sine, cosine and tangent of (a) in **degrees**
sinpi(a), cospi(a)	sine, cosine of (πa) with (a) in **radians**
asin(a), acos(a), atan(a)	inverse sine, cosine and tangent of (a) in **radians**
asind(a), acosd(a), atand(a)	inverse sine, cosine and tangent of (a) in **degrees**
atan(y,x), atand(y,x)	inverse tangent of y/x in radians, degrees
sec(a), csc(a), cot(a)	secant, cosecant, cotangent of (a) in **radians**
secd(a), cscd(a), cotd(a)	secant, cosecant, cotangent of (a) in **degrees**
asec(a), acsc(a), acot(a)	inverse sec, cosecant, cotangent of (a) in **radians**
asecd(a), acscd(a), acotd(a)	inverse sec, cosecant, cotangent of (a) in **degrees**
sech(a), csch(a), coth(a)	hyperbolic sec, cosecant, cotangent of (a) in **radians**
asinh(a), acosh(a), atanh(a)	inverse hyperbolic sine, cosine, tangent of (a) in **radians**
asech(a), acsch(a), acoth(a)	inverse hyperbolic sec, cosecant, cotangent of (a) in **radians**
sinc(x)	$\sin(\pi x) / \pi x$ for x≠0 or 1 if x=0
cosc(x)	$\cos(\pi x)/x - \sin(\pi x) / (\pi x^2)$ for x≠0 or 0 if x=0
deg2rad(a), rad2deg(a)	convert (a) to or from radians to degrees

5.4 - Boolean Comparisons

Boolean Comparison Operators	
a == b	a is equal to b
a === b	a is identical to b
a != b or a ≠ b	a is not equal to b
a > b	a is greater than b
a >= b or a ≥ b	a is greater than or equal to b
a < b	a is less than b
a <= b or a ≤ b	a is less than or equal to b
cmp(a, b)	-1 if a<b, 0 if a=b, +1 if a> b
!b	not b
&&	Boolean AND
||	Boolean OR

The result of a Boolean comparison is a Bool variable equal to "true"or "false".

```
julia> x = 2.5
julia> y = 5.6

julia> x > y
false

julia> x < y
true
```

Multiple simple comparisons can be concatenated into a compound comparison using the && (and) and II (or) operators:

```
julia> z = 10.0

julia> (x < y) && (z > y)        # parentheses are not required
true

julia> (x < y) && (z < y)        # parentheses are not required
false
```

Many other special mathematical functions are provided by the package "SpecialFunctions". Packages are discussed next.

5.5 - Julia Packages

The base Julia installation provides dozens of elementary functions as described in the previous sections. But there are also thousands of other more complex functions that are available by importing code "packages". Each package contains functions related to a specific topic, for example Statistics, Sorting, and so forth. There are over 2000 registered packages so I will mention only a few.

Packages are imported using the Package Manager (pkg). At the Julia prompt in the REPL, start by typing a right-bracket:

```
julia> ]                         # launch pkg by typing ]
(v1.0) pkg> add Statistics       # "add" the desired package
.
.                 # a long delay while the package is downloaded and compiled
.
(v1.0) pkg>                      # leave pkg by pressing delete
julia>
julia> using Statistics          # make "Statistics" available to Julia


julia> x = [1,2,3,4,5,6,7,8,9]
julia> mean(x)                   # mean() is part of the Statistics package
5.0

julia> std(x)                    # std() is part of the Statistics package
2.7386127875258306
```

The mean, and std (standard deviation) functions are made available by adding the Statistics package.

In the Jupyter Notebook environment, the syntax for adding a Julia package is slightly different:

```
In [5]:  import Pkg
         Pkg.add("Calculus")
         using Calculus

         derivative(sin,0.0)


Out[5]:  0.9999999999938886
```

Without "adding" and "using" the "Calculus" package, the call to derivative() would have generated an "undefined" error.

There are a few other things you can do in the pkg mode. Using the "up" command will cause the pkg manager to update all of the installed packages:

```
(v1.0) pkg> up
  Updating registry at `~/.julia/registries/General`
  Updating git-repo `https://github.com/JuliaRegistries/General.git`
  Updating `~/.julia/environments/v1.0/Project.toml`
  Updating `~/.julia/environments/v1.0/Manifest.toml`
```

Using "status" in pkg mode will list all of the packages you have installed:

```
(v1.0) pkg> status
  [336ed68f] CSV v0.4.2
  [a93c6f00] DataFrames v0.14.1
  [59287772] Formatting v0.3.4
  [7073ff75] IJulia v1.13.0
  [429524aa] Optim v0.17.1
  [d330b81b] PyPlot v2.6.3
  [8bb1440f] DelimitedFiles
  [37e2e46d] LinearAlgebra
  [9a3f8284] Random
  [10745b16] Statistics
```

So, how do you find a package or even if there is a package that does something you need to do? Fortunately, there is a website that tries to keep up with the ever evolving world of packages:

https://juliaobserver.com/ .

Julia Observer provides lists of popular packages and it organizes packages into categories making it easier to find a desired package if it exists. For example on the next page is a list of the 20 most popular Julia packages of all time.

The number of stars indicates the number of users who have "liked" that particular package.

The most popular package, IJulia, has been mentioned previously. It is the link between Julia and the Jupyter Notebook environment.

Gadfly provides statistical graphics for Julia. Mocha is a deep learning framework for Julia. And so forth.

Top twenty all-time

IJulia	★ 1296	↑ 10
Gadfly	★ 1180	↑ 2
Mocha	★ 1054	↑ 2
Knet	★ 598	↑ 5
DifferentialEquations	★ 539	↑ 8
Plots	★ 523	↑ 8
JuMP	★ 514	↑ 6
DataFrames	★ 491	↑ 0
PyCall	★ 451	↑ 3
DSGE	★ 421	↑ 2
Flux	★ 406	↑ 16
TensorFlow	★ 359	↑ 10
Cxx	★ 354	↑ 2
Distributions	★ 319	↑ 1
Optim	★ 315	↑ 4
MXNet	★ 307	↑ 2
Turing	★ 249	↑ 6
Convex	★ 225	↑ 1
Interact	★ 220	↑ 0

These are the 20 most popular packages. A complete list of all 2000 Julia packages can be found at

https://pkg.julialang.org/

This list is arranged more or less in alphabetical order so it might be helpful to first find your package name using the JuliaObserver site.

Using the "StatsBase" package as an example: Find "StatsBase" in the list of all Julia packages at the pkg.julialang.org site. Click on the StatsBase name in the list.

That will take you to another page devoted to the StatsBase package as illustrated below. Click on the "docs-stable" button shown outlined.

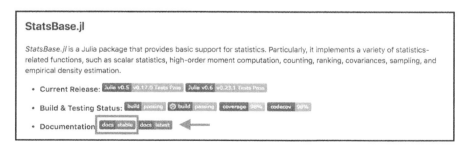

That will take you to the documentation for the functions in the StatsBase package as illustrated on the next page. You should be able to determine using this documentation whether or not to use the package or to start over with a new package from the pkg.julialang.org list.

Documentation for the StatsBase Package

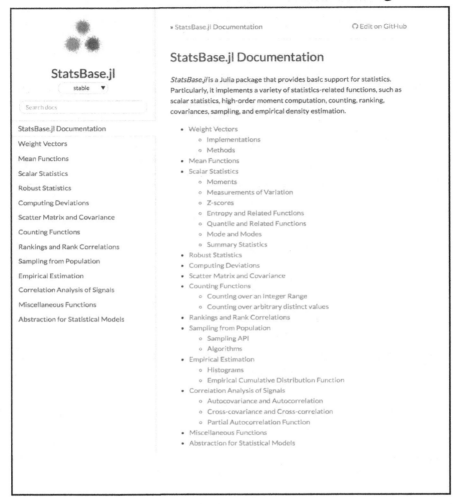

Julia packages, and indeed Julia itself, are being developed by volunteers and teams. Because of this the quality of the package itself and of the documentation that goes with the package will vary from package to package. If there is more than one package that might satisfy your requirements, it would perhaps be prudent to start with the package that has the highest number of stars.

"import" vs "using":

A julia package can be included in the current code using either "import" or "using". What's the difference?

- **"import"** - if you "import" a package, you must prefix the name of the functions in that package with the name of the package itself. This is a good way to avoid name collisions between functions with the same name from different packages.

> **Calculus**.derivative(cos, pi)

- **"using"** - If you import a package using "using", then you don't need to prefix the function name with the package name:

> derivative(cos, pi)

Up to now, we have been discussing functions that are supplied as part of the base Julia installation, or that are available from add-on packages. Now it is time to discuss writing your own code.

5.6 - Function Names

Functions are named, self contained blocks of Julia code that perform a specific action. When a function is called, it is provided with a set of input arguments. The function code operates on these inputs and returns the result. For example, here's a function that doubles the input

```
julia> function fa(a)
          return 2a
      end
fa (generic function with 1 method)


julia> fa(3)
6
```

By convention names of functions are in lower case, without underscores. A simple function name might be **fxy()** . The parentheses are used by Julia to recognize that **fxy** is a function and not a variable.

Input arguments to the function are contained within the parentheses separated using commas. For example: **fxy**(x,y) where the function **fxy** accepts the input variables x and y and returns some value or values computed from those variables.

Functions can return more than one variable:

```
julia> function fxy(x,y)
          v = 2x
          w = 3y
          return v,w
      end
fxy (generic function with 1 method)

julia> fxy(3,4)
(6, 12)
```

If one or more of the function's input arguments are mutable, then the function can modify the value of that variable and this modification will exist outside the function. By convention, the name of a function that modifies the value of one or more of it's input arguments ends with an exclamation point: **fxy!**(x,y). See the section "Mutable vs Immutable" a little later.

5.7 - Simple Function Forms

Julia provides several different ways in which a function can be written. For example, here is a simple function that accepts two arguments, x and y, and returns a single value equal to (2*x+3*y). The name of this function is "**fxy()**":

```
julia> function fxy(x, y)        # the word "function" is required
           return(2*x+3*y)       # "return", *,  and ( ) are optional
       end                       # end is required

julia> fxy(2,3)                  # evaluate fxy for x=2 and y=3
13
```

This syntax would be appropriate for complex functions that contain many statements. The function definition begins with the word "function" and ends with the word "end". If you are typing this in the REPL, you will notice that you can hit "return" or "enter" to space down one line while still staying in the function definition. The definition does not end until Julia finds the word "end".

This "verbose" syntax is clear and unambiguous. Julia also allows a more compact syntax that leaves out "return" and parentheses:

```
julia> function fxy(x, y)
           2*x+3*y               # the * can also be omitted => 2x + 3y
       end

julia> fxy(2,3)
13
```

By default Julia returns the value of the last statement evaluated when "end" is reached. So it is possible to leave out the word "return" with the understanding that it will be the result of the last expression that will be returned.

For simple functions it is possible to be even more concise:

```
julia> fxy(x, y) = 2x+3y

julia> fxy(2,3)
13
```

Notice that the words "function" and "end" are not used. The character sequence **fXY(** is recognized by Julia as the beginning of a function definition. This syntax is called the "assignment form" of a function definition. It can only be used if the function contains only a single expression.

5.8 - Begin Blocks

Sometime it is necessary to evaluate several expressions before computing the final returned value. A "begin Block" syntax allows this.

```
julia> fxy(x,y) = begin
                    z = 2x
                    w = 3y
                    z + w
            end
julia> fxy(2,3)
13
```

A simple begin block can be written in a single line using semicolons:

```
julia> fxy(x,y) = begin z = 2x; w = 3y; z + w end
julia> fxy(5,6)
28
```

5.9 - Chain Syntax

It is possible to combine several statements into a single line using semicolons to separate individual statements without using parentheses and omitting the begin and end keywords:

```
julia> fxy(x,y) = (z=2x; w=3y; z+w)
julia> fxy(5,6)
28
```

The chain syntax can also be written on multiple lines:

```
julia> fxy(x,y) = (z=2x;
                    w=3y;
                    z+w)
julia> fxy(5,6)
28
```

5.10 - Scope of Variables

Every variable exists in a "scope". That variable is "visible" inside its scope, but is "invisible" outside that scope. Every code block creates a new scope and variables defined within that code block can be used inside that code block, but will not be visible outside that code block. Code blocks can be defined by functions, and by "for" and "while" loops. Basically any code block that ends with "end" defines a new scope.

For nested code blocks, variables defined in the superior block will be visible inside inferior blocks contained inside the superior block. For example, variables defined at the top level of code will be visible to any code blocks inside that top level.

Perhaps the pseudo-code on the next page will help clarify scopes:

```
01   # start of code
02   define variable "a"
03   function f()
04          variable "a" is visible
05          define variable "b"
06          for i in 1:10
07                    variables "a" and "b" are visible
08                    define variable "c"
09          end # for loop
10          variables "a" and "b" are visible
11          variable "c" is not visible
12   end # function f()
13   variable "a" is visible
14   variables "b" and "c" are not visible
```

Conflicting variable names can cause code to crash and can be very difficult to track down. There are a couple of ways to avoid variable name conflicts:

- Prefix the name of a local variable with an underscore (_). This defines that variable name to be local to the scope in which it is defined:

```
julia> for i in 1:3
           _a = 5                 # _a is only valid inside this for loop
           println(_a + i)
       end
6
7
8

julia> _a
ERROR: UndefVarError: _a not defined
```

- Use the keyword "**global**" to define a variable inside an inferior scope to refer to the variable with that same name in a superior scope.

```
julia> x = 2          # variable x is defined in the global scope

julia> function f()
           global x = 6      # this "x" is the same "x" definded above
       end

julia> f()            # run f() which redefines "x"

julia> x
6                     # global "x" has been redefined = 6
```

Use the keyword "**local**" to define a variable that is only visible in the local scope.

```
julia> function f()
          x = 0         # this x is visible inside f() but outside the for loop
          for i in 1:3
            local x     # this x is visible only inside the for loop
            x = i
            println(x)  # prints the x inside the for loop
          end # for loop
          println(x)    # print the x visible outside the for loop
       end # f()

julia> f()
1                       # these are the values of the local x inside the for loop
2                       # these are the values of the local x inside the for loop
3                       # these are the values of the local x inside the for loop

0                       # this is the value of the x outsode the for loop
```

• Avoid using the same name for variables that you intend to be not the same variable.

5.11 - Anonymous Functions

An example of the syntax for defining an anonymous function is:

```
julia> x->2x^2
#8 (generic function with 1 method)
```

But this form is useless because, since the function has no name, it cannot be called and thus cannot be executed. The utility of an anonymous function is as an argument for a function that expects to accept a function as one of its arguments. There are several such cases. Two such cases are the map() function and array "comprehension":

5.10.1 - The Map Function:

The map function takes two arguments: an array and a function that operates on each element of that array.

```
julia> array = 1:4                        # define a 4 element array
1:4

julia> new_array = map(x->2x^2, array)    # map array to new_array
4-element Array{Int64,1}:
  2
  8
 18
 32
```

The map function creates a new_array where each element of the new array is given by: new_array[i] = 2*array[i]^2

```
julia> array[3]              # the original array is unchanged
3

julia> new_array[3]          # the new array is computed based on array
18
```

5.10.2 - Array Comprehension:

An array comprehension is a method for creating an array based on a function of each element in an existing array. The syntax is similar to that of an anonymous function but without the "x->". For example

```
julia> new_array = [2x^2 for x in array]
4-element Array{Int64,1}:
  2
  8
 18
 32

julia> new_array[4]
32
```

5.12 - Mutable vs Immutable

Normally functions do not change the values of their input arguments. In fact, if the input argument is of an immutable Type, then the function cannot change the value of that argument. For example here is a function that appears to change the value of its input argument x:

```
julia> function fx!(x)
           x=20              # function fx!(x) attempts to redefine the value of x
       end
fx (generic function with 1 method)

julia> x = 10                # set x=10 outside the function
10

julia> fx!(x)                # run the function which returns 20
20

julia> x
10                           # but the value of x outside the function has not changed
```

There are functions that can change the value of one or more of their input arguments and these functions have names that, by convention, end with an exclamation point ! . It should be noted that the exclamation point symbol, ! , has no "power" to allow the function to modify its input arguments. It is simply an indication that the function might change the value of one or more of its input arguments.

Functions can only modify the values of input arguments if those arguments are of a "mutable" Type. For example, arrays are mutable. The array itself cannot be changed but the values contained in that array can be changed.

```
julia> x = [2 3 4]        # define a simple array x[ ]
1×3 Array{Int64,2}:
 2  3  4

julia> x[2]               # before calling the function the value of x[2] = 3
3

julia> function fx!(a)    # here's a function that changes the value of a[2]
          a[2] = 10
       end
fx! (generic function with 1 method)

julia> fx!(x)             # run function fx! with the array x as input

julia> x[2]               # the value of x[2] has been changed outside the function
10
```

There is a built-in function, "isimmutable()", that will return "true" if the argument is immutable. This might help you figure out why your code is not working the way you expected.

```
julia> y=3

julia> isimmutable(y)         # "true" means the external value of y cannot
true                          # be changed from inside a function

julia> x = [2 3 4]            # create a simple array
1×3 Array{Int64,2}:
 2  3  4

julia> isimmutable(x)         # false means the external values contained in
false                         # array x can be changed from inside a function
```

An immutable object is passed in assignment statements and in function calls by copying. Changing the copy does not change the original. A mutable object is passed by pointer to the memory location. Changing the object at that location changes the original

5.13 - Methods & Multiple Dispatch

A Julia function might have several different data Types as input arguments. For example, consider the simple asterisk operator ' * '. Typically this operator would multiply two numerical data Types. But those data types might be Float64, Int32, Complex32 or any combination of these Types. The asterisk operator must have different code implementations to handle all possible combination of input Types. These different code implementations are referred to as "Methods".

There is a Julia function that lists all of the methods available for a given function or operator. This list is created by executing methods(name_of_function). For example:

```
julia> methods(*)
# 343 methods for generic function "*":
[1] *(x::Bool, z::Complex{Bool}) in Base at complex.jl:281
[2] *(x::Bool, y::Bool) in Base at bool.jl:106
[3] *(x::Bool, y::T) where T<:AbstractFloat in Base at bool.jl:118
```

[4] *(x::Bool, z::Complex) in Base at complex.jl:288
[5] *(x::Bool, y::AbstractIrrational) in Base at irrationals.jl:135
[6] *(a::Float16, b::Float16) in Base at float.jl:392
[7] *(x::Float32, y::Float32) in Base at float.jl:398
[8] *(x::Float64, y::Float64) in Base at float.jl:399

There are 343 different methods needed to implement the simple ' * ' operator. Only the first 8 are shown here. Each method accepts a different combination of input argument Types. Julia has to decide which of these methods to use depending upon the data Types of the arguments. This process of deciding which Method to use is called "Multiple Dispatch" and it is one of Julia's most powerful features.

5.14 - Macros

Macros are similar to functions in that they contain a block of code that gets executed by invoking the name of the macro. Macro names always begin with the "at" character, @. Julia handles macros entirely differently than functions. Functions are parsed and compiled at compile time. Macros are compiled at run time. This is because macros are used primarily for meta programming - writing code that generates code that gets compiled and executed at run time. Unless you intend to do meta programming, you probably will have no need to write a macro. In fact, the Julia Style Guidelines suggest that if your objective can be met with a function or a macro, then use the function. Code within a function generally runs faster than the same code in a macro.

Macros are written just as if they were functions but with the keyword 'macro" instead of "function". For example:

```
julia> macro mxy(x,y)
    z = x+y
    print("$x + $y = $z")
    end
@mxy (macro with 1 method)

julia> @mxy(4,5)
4 + 5 = 9
```

Notice that the macro is written without the @ symbol. The @ symbol is used to execute the macro.

Even though you may never have to write a macro, there are some macros supplied as part of the standard Julia installation that you might find useful.

Here are a few of the macros available in Julia that might be useful. You can find help on these and other macros by typing ?@macroName in the REPL.

- **@assert condition [text]**

    Throw an AssertionError if condition is false. "text" is optionally displayed upon assertion failure.

    ```
    julia> @assert iseven(3) ["3 is not even"]
    ERROR: AssertionError: [3 is not even]
    ```

This can be easier to use than doing the testing yourself.

There are two macros that allow you to measure execution times:

- **@elapsed**

  A macro to evaluate an expression returning the number of seconds it took to execute the expression.

  ```
  julia> ft(i) = begin          # define a simple function
              for n=1:10000
                   i=i+1
              end
              print(i)
         end
  ```

  ```
  julia> @elapsed ft(1)         # find the time to execute the function
  10001  1.5496e-5
  ```

There is a second timer macro that appears to be very similar to @elapsed:

- **@time**

  A macro to execute an expression, printing the time it took to execute.

  ```
  julia> @time ft(1)
  10001  0.000026 seconds (8 allocations: 288 bytes)
  ```

Run the same function a second time:

  ```
  julia> @time ft(1)
  10001  0.000017 seconds (8 allocations: 288 bytes)
  ```

Notice that it took less time to execute the second time. This is because some of the behind the scenes work was done the first time the function was evaluated.

Don't confuse the macro **@time** with the function **time()**. The function **time()** returns the current time whereas the macro **@time** returns elapsed time for execution of some code block.

Two more macros that might be useful:

- **@label name**

  Labels a statement with the symbolic label name. The label marks the end-point of an unconditional jump with @goto name.

- **@goto name**

  @goto name unconditionally jumps to the statement at the location @label name.

5.15 - Using Keywords in Argument Lists

Some functions have several arguments and sometimes it is difficult to remember what order they were specified in the function definition. To avoid this problem, it is possible to name Julia function arguments.

Named arguments must come after all unnamed arguments and must be separated from them by a semicolon. For example, here is a function that takes three arguments: an unnamed number "x", a named argument "power" and a named argument "divisor'. Note that it is possible to specify default values for the named arguments. In this case the default value for power = 2 and for divisor = 3.0:

```
julia> function fpower(x; power=2, divisor=3.0)
       return (x^power)/divisor
       end
fpower (generic function with 1 method)
```

```
julia> fpower(4)              # if values for named parameters are not
5.333333333333333             # specified, then the default values are used
```

```
julia> fpower(4, power=3)     # it is not required to specify all values
21.333333333333332
```

```
julia> fpower(4, divisor=10, power=3)
6.4
```

You must specify values for all of the **un**named arguments in the same order as in the function definition but assigning values to named arguments is optional. Named arguments can be listed in any order not just the order in which they were defined. If no value is given for a named argument, then the default value specified in the function definition is used.

5.16 - Functions with Optional Arguments

It is possible to specify optional arguments in a function definition. Optional arguments are given a default value which is used if the function call does not define a different value for that argument. This is similar to keyword arguments as described in the previous section, except that optional arguments do not have to be named. Optional arguments are identified by the presence of a default value.

```
julia> function abc(a=1, b=2, c=3)
          println("a = $a")
          println("b = $b")
          println("c = $c")
       end
abc (generic function with 4 methods)
```

```
julia> abc()          # with no argument values the default values are used
a = 1
b = 2
c = 3
```

```
julia> abc(2,3,4)     # argument values override the default values
a = 2
b = 3
c = 4
```

```
julia> abc(2)          # arguments are identified by their position in the arg list
a = 2                  # the first argument is assigned to the variable "a"
b = 2
c = 3
```

It is important to note that these are not named arguments. Trying to input argument values as if they were key-value pairs results in an error.

```
julia> abc(c=4)
ERROR: function abc does not accept keyword arguments
```

5.17 - Functions with Variable Number of Arguments

Some functions can accept a variable number of arguments. The variable arguments are indicated by an ellipsis (**...**) which is typed as three periods. The ellipsis must be the last item in the argument list.

```
julia> function anyargs(args...)
           for arg in args
               println(arg)
           end
       end
anyargs (generic function with 1 method)

julia> anyargs(3, "Sam",4.5)
3
Sam
4.5
```

In the function definition, anyargs(**args...**), the ellipsis must be preceded by some name, "args" in this case, so that the function has a name to use to reference the arguments. The ellipsis can represent any number of arguments including no arguments.

5.18 - Multiple Return Values

If you need to return multiple values from a function, package them as a Tuple and return the Tuple.

```
julia> function powers(x)
           x2 = x^2
           x3 = x^3
           x4 = x^4
           return (x2, x3, x4)
       end

julia> p = powers(2)
(4, 8, 16)

julia> typeof(p)
Tuple{Int64,Int64,Int64}
```

5.19 - Strange Symbols

In addition to the standard math symbols shown in the previous "Math Functions" table, Julia also uses some other symbols that may be unfamiliar to you:

::Type

The double colon symbol is used to specify the Type of variables and expressions. For example, :: can be used to restrict the Type of arguments for a function:

```
julia> f(x::Float64) = 2x
f (generic function with 1 method)
```

This function will only accept a variable of Type Float64.

```
julia> f(2.0)          # this will work since 2.0 is Type Float64
4.0

julia> f(2)            # this will not work since 2 is not Type Float64
ERROR: MethodError: no method matching f(::Int64)
```

You should avoid using the :: syntax unless there is a specific reason to require a specific Type for a variable.

The :: syntax can be used to test the type of a variable

```
julia> x = 5::Int       # this Type assertion is true
5

julia> x = 5.0::Int     # this Type assertion is false and generates an error
ERROR: TypeError: in typeassert, expected Int64, got Float64
```

|>

This symbol "pipes" the output of one function to the input of another function.

```
julia> 1:10 |> sum |> sqrt
7.416198487095663
```

The range 1:10 is passed to the sum() function and that sum is passed to the sqrt() function.

=>

This symbol is used with Key-Value pairs such as used in Dictionaries to specify the value of an item identified by a Key.

Dict("name1"=>"Joe")   # name1 is the key and Joe is the value

----

x->

This symbol is used to begin the definition of an "anonymous function" as described in a previous section: **map(x->2x^2, array)**.

Chapter 6

Tuples

In the previous chapter we discussed individual items of data. But there are frequently collections of data items that are related to one another and it is convenient for the programmer to organize these data into a structure that makes visualizing the data easier. Julia implements several different data structures to accommodate these cases.

The simplest data structure is a "tuple". An n-tuple is a sequence of n elements separated by commas and optionally enclosed in parentheses ( ). Tuples can contain any types of data, but those data types cannot be modified once created. Tuples can be accessed via indexing using standard [ ] indexing:

```
julia> t = (1, "Joe")     # Tuple t contains one Int64 number and one string
(1, "Joe")

julia> typeof(t)
Tuple{Int64,String}     # the type of t is "Tuple"

julia> t[1]             # index 1 is the first item in the Tuple
1

julia> t[2]             # index 2 is the second item in the Tuple
"Joe"
```

Data items in a Tuple can also be named creating a "Named Tuple". Items in a Named Tuple can be addressed using indexing or by name using a dot notation:

```
julia> named = (member=1, name="Joe")       # data items are named
julia> named[2]       # data items can be addressed by standard indexing
"Joe"

julia> named.name   # data items can also be addressed by name
"Joe"
```

Tuples can also be constructed without the parentheses. Data items separated by commas are assumed to compose a tuple.

```
julia> noParens = 1, "Joe"     # tuple constructed without parentheses
julia> typeof(noParens)
Tuple{Int64,String}
```

```
julia> noParens[2]
"Joe"
```

Many functions return more than a single value. For example, this function accepts a single value and returns two values:

```
julia> function f1(x)
          return (x^2, x^3) # function f1 returns two values packaged as a tuple
       end

julia> f1(2)
(4, 8)                  # the two return values are packaged as a tuple

julia> y, z = f1(2)     # the returned tuple can be deconstructed
julia> y                # into individual values y
4

julia> z                # and z
8
```

Because tuples can be constructed without parentheses, it is possible to write a function return statement in several different ways. These all return the same values:

```
julia> function f1(x)
          return (x^2, x^3) # function f1 returns two values packaged as a tuple
       end

julia> function f2(x)
          return x^2, x^3  # the return tuple can be written without parentheses
       end

julia> function f3(x)
          x^2, x^3         # the return tuple can be written without "return"
       end
```

Tuples can also be used in function argument lists:

```
julia> p = 'a','b','c'  # a tuple constructed without parentheses
('a', 'b', 'c')         # Julia supplies the parentheses

julia> typeof(p)        # typeof confirms that p is a tuple containing characters
Tuple{Char,Char,Char}

julia> println(p)       # the tuple p can be passed to the function println
('a', 'b', 'c')

julia> function pp(p)   # function pp takes a tuple as input
          d = p[1]      # the tuple can be deconstructed using indices
          e = p[2]
          f = p[3]
          println(d,e,f) # d,e, and f are separate data items (characters)
       end

julia> pp(p)            # the function pp is passed the tuple p as input
abc                     # and outputs the components of that tuple
```

Chapter 7

Data Arrays

In the previous chapter we introduced the Tuple, a simple 1-dimensional data structure. In this chapter we will expand our discussion to include multi-dimensional data arrays. Most of the discussion will use 1 and 2-dimensional arrays as examples, but the material presented also applies to arrays with more than 2-dimensions.

2-Dimensional Array

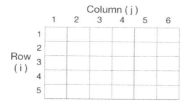

3-Dimensional Array

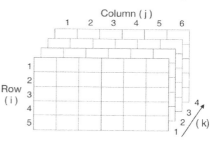

The figure above illustrates a 2-dimensional and a 3-dimensional array. The 2-dimensional array is indexed by specifying the row and column number (row,col) of the desired data item. The letters i and j are frequently used to represent the row and column number (i, j). A 3-dimensional array is composed of a set of 2-dimensional arrays all with the same number of rows and columns as illustrated at the right in the figure. In this case a specific data item is indexed as (row,col,matrix), frequently described as (i, j, k).

7.1 - Vector, Matrix, and Array:

"Vector", "Matrix", and "Array" are different names for the same type of data structure. With Julia, the basic data structure is an "Array". An Array is an N-dimensional collection of data. A "Vector" is a 1-dimensional Array. A "Matrix" is a 2-dimensional Array. This is illustrated by the figure below.

The term "dimension" is used differently depending upon which name is used to refer to an array. A "Vector" is a 1-dimensional array that consists of a single column of real numbers. The Vector illustrated at the right is a 5-dimension Vector, but only a single dimension Array. This is further illustrated by the figure on the next page.

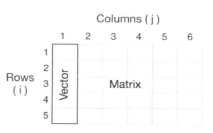

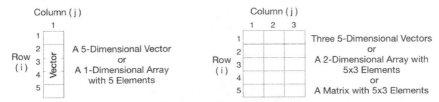

The Type names "Vector" and "Matrix" have the advantage of being unambiguous. They also make vector and matrix operations more familiar. However, Julia uses the type name "Array" for all array types regardless of the number of dimensions. If you define a data structure of Type "Vector," Julia will automatically convert it into an "Array{Type,1}"

Vector{Type} is an alias for **Array**{Type,1}:

> julia> **Vector**{Int64} == **Array**{Int64,1}   # a **1**-dimensional array
> **true**

Similarly, **Matrix**{Type} is an alias for **Array**{Type,2}

> julia> **Matrix**{Int64} == **Array**{Int64,2} # a **2**-dimensional array
> **true**

7.2 - Creating Vectors:

Create a Vector using the syntax Vector{Type}. It will be a 1-dimensional array by definition. Vectors are strictly arrays of real numbers (Float64), but Julia allows Array elements to be of Any Type.

> julia> v1 = **Vector**{Int64}   # create an Int64 Type Vector
> Array{Int64,1}

You can then fill the Vector by enumerating its contents:

> julia> v1 = [1;2;3]   # use semicolons to separate elements
> 3-element Array{Int64,1}:
> 1
> 2
> 3

The Vector components can be indexed using a single number because a Vector is a 1-dimensional array by definition.

> julia> v1[2]
> 2

You can also create a Vector with a specified number of elements and fill that Vector with undefined data:

> julia> v = Vector(**undef**,5)   # create a Vector with 5 dimensions
> 5-element Array{Any,1}:
> #undef
> #undef

```
#undef
#undef
#undef
```

Remember that a 5 element Vector is also called a 5-**dimensional** Vector

7.3 - Creating Matrices:

Create a Matrix using the syntax Matrix{Type}. A Matrix is a 2-dimensional array of n by m elements where "n" is the number of rows and "m" is the number of columns:

```
julia> m1 = Matrix{Float64}    # declare the Type of data
Array{Float64,2}               # a Matrix is a 2-dimensional array by definition
```

You can then fill the Matrix

```
julia> m1 = [1 2 3; 4 5 6]     # columns separated by spaces
2×3 Array{Int64,2}:            # rows separated by semicolons
 1  2  3
 4  5  6
```

This creates a 2 row by 3 column 2-dimensional Matrix.

You can also create an n by m Matrix filled with undefined data by using:

```
julia> m = Matrix(undef, 4, 5)   # create a 4x5 2-dim Matrix
4×5 Array{Any,2}:
#undef #undef #undef #undef #undef
#undef #undef #undef #undef #undef
#undef #undef #undef #undef #undef
#undef #undef #undef #undef #undef
```

7.4 - Punctuation Matters

One way to create a new array is to list the data the array is to contain enclosed in square brackets. For example:

```
julia> a = [10; 20; 30]        # semicolons separate rows
```

This statement will create a 1-dimensional column array containing 3 elements.

When creating a new Array by enumerating the data the new Array is to contain, it is important to pay attention to the punctuation used to separate the data items.

The statement shown above with data elements separated by **semicolons** produces a 1-dimensional **column** array (Vector):

```
julia> a = [10; 20; 30]        # semicolons separate rows
3-element Array{Int64,1}:
 10
 20
 30
```

Data separated by **spaces** produces a 2-dimensional **row** array:

```
julia> b = [10 20 30]          # spaces separate columns
1×3 Array{Int64,2}:
```

55

| 10 20 30

Combining the **space** separated columns and the **semicolon** separated rows yields a 2-dimensional array with more than one row:

```
julia> c = [10 20 30 ; 40 50 60]
2×3 Array{Int64,2}:
 10 20 30
 40 50 60
```

It is also possible to create a 1-dimensional column array (Vector) by separating the rows with commas:

```
julia> a = [10, 20, 30]
3-element Array{Int64,1}:
 10
 20
 30
```

However, this could lead to problems for multidimensional arrays where it is not permitted to combine commas and semicolons in the same statement. It is best to follow these "rules":

- Use semicolons to separate rows of data
- Use spaces to separate columns of data

7.5 - Creating Arrays:

An "Array" is an ordered collection of elements as illustrated in the previous figures. Those elements can be any of the basic data types that have been previously described: integer, floating point number, Boolean, character, or string. Each element in an array is addressed by an "index" consisting of a list of numbers separated by commas and enclosed in square brackets. For a 2-dimensional array the index contains the row and column number of the element so, for example, array[2,5] refers to the contents of the cell in **row** 2 and **column** 5.

There are many different ways to create an array. The first is simply to enumerate the items that make up the array as illustrated above and here.

```
julia> a = [1.0; 2.0]              # square brackets indicate an Array
2-element Array{Float64,1}:        # "1" is the number of dimensions in the Array
 1.0
 2.0
```

Notice that Julia has deduced the data Type the array a contains (Float64).

Generally all the items in an Array column are of the same type, but Julia allows any type of data to be used for each item in an Array:

```
julia> b = [1, 'C', 6.2, "string"]
4-element Array{Any,1}:
 1
 'C'
 6.2
 "string"
```

When the items in an Array are not all of the same type, the data type for the Array itself is "**Any**" meaning that the Array can contain any type of data.

If an Array, when it is created is empty, that is it does not contain any data from which Julia can deduce a data type, then it is necessary to specify what type of data the array is intended to contain. To create a 3-dim Array of 2x2-dim arrays:

```
julia> s = Array{Int64}(undef, 2, 2, 2)    # create two 2x2 dim Arrays
2×2×2 Array{Int64,3}:                        # containing Int64 data

[:, :, 1] =                                  # the first 2x2 dim Array
 4566949896  4792958768                      # the data elements are undefined
 4792958736  4792958800                      # filled with left over garbage

[:, :, 2] =                                  # the second 2x2 dim Array
 4792958832  4794207952
 4792958864  4794426848
```

Creating a simple 1-dim Array uses a simpler syntax. Because no array size is specified, it is assumed to be a 1-dim array:

```
julia> g = Float64[ ]            # Array g can contain only Float64 data
0-element Array{Float64,1}

julia> h = Any[ ]                # Array h can contain any type of data
0-element Array{Any,1}
```

Items can be added to the end of an existing array using the **push!** function:

```
julia> s = [ ]                   # s is an empty array
0-element Array{Any,1}

julia> push!(s, 5.0)             # push the number 5.0 onto the end of s
1-element Array{Any,1}:
 5.0
```

By default **push!** pushes an element onto the end of the array. It is also possible to push a new element onto the front of an array using **pushfirst!**. The new element becomes the element at index = 1 and the existing items move down one index.

```
julia> pushfirst!(s,10.0)        # push the number 10.0 into the 1st index
2-element Array{Any,1}:
 10.0
 5.0
```

It is also possible to insert an item into any location in an existing array using **insert!**. The item being inserted becomes the element at the specified index. The existing elements "move aside" to make room for the new element:

```
julia> insert!(s, 2, 7.5)        # insert 7.5 into array s at index 2
 10.0
 7.5
 5.0
```

The **append!** function can also be used to add items to the end of an existing array. Using the previously defined Array "s" as an example, we will append an Array "t":

```
julia> t = [6,7,8]
 6
 7
 8

julia> append!(s,t)          # append! "t" to the end of "s"
10.0
 7.5
 5.0
 6
 7
 8
```

The advantage of using **push!** and **append!** to fill an array is that the array is never larger than it needs to be, but if you know ahead of creation time how large the array needs to be then it is better to create an array that size using one of the following functions.

If you want an empty array of specified size, you can do this:

```
julia> a = Array{Int64}(undef, 3)        # create a 1-dim Array with 3 elements
3-element Array{Int64,1}:
 4731614320                               # the array is filled with garbage
 4731614384                               # left in memory by previous
 4731614416                               # operations

julia> twoD = Array{Int64}(undef,2,3)
2×3 Array{Int64,2}:
 2 47   1        # this is an array with 2 rows and 3 columns
 1  3  88        # filled with Int64 garbage
```

Julia can create arrays of a specified size filled with numbers:

```
julia> k = Array{Float64}(5:9)    # create an array filled with numbers 5 to 9
5-element Array{Float64,1}:
 5.0
 6.0
 7.0
 8.0
 9.0                              # unlike Python, Julia includes the final element
julia> k[2]                       # the resulting array is filled with Float64 numbers
 6.0
```

Julia has built-in functions to create Arrays filled with specific numbers:

```
julia> z = zeros(Float64,3)      # fills a new array of size 3 with zeros
3-element Array{Float64,1}:
 0.0
 0.0
 0.0
```

```
julia> F = ones(Int64,2,3)        # fills a new array of size 2x3 with ones
2×3 Array{Int64,2}:
 1  1  1
 1  1  1
```

```
julia> F = fill("Sam",3)          # fills a new Array of size 3 with "Sam"
3-element Array{String,1}:
 "Sam"
 "Sam"
 "Sam"
```

It is also possible to create a new array filled with Boolean values:

```
julia> boolArray = trues(2,3)
2×3 BitArray{2}:
 true  true  true
 true  true  true
```

All of these functions can create multi-dimensional arrays:

```
julia> zeros(2,3,2)               # create a 3-dimensional array
2×3×2 Array{Float64,3}:
[:, :, 1] =
 0.0  0.0  0.0
 0.0  0.0  0.0

[:, :, 2] =
 0.0  0.0  0.0
 0.0  0.0  0.0
```

The function **fill!** with an exclamation point (**!**) fills an **existing** array. The previous contents of the array are erased.

```
julia> fill!(F,"Bill")            # fills an existing array with "Bill"
3-element Array{String,1}:
 "Bill"
 "Bill"
 "Bill"
```

Julia can make a copy of an existing array using the **copy** function: Using the array "F" from the previous example as a template:

```
julia> h = copy(F)
3-element Array{String,1}:
 "Bill"
 "Bill"
 "Bill"
```

Julia can also create a new array "**similar**" to an exiting array:

```
julia> g = similar(F)
3-element Array{String,1}:
  #undef                        # the "similar" Array is filled with undefined data
  #undef
  #undef
```

"**Similar**" creates a new array with the same dimensions and data type as the template but this new array contains whatever bits were in the allocated memory when the similar array was created - basically garbage.

Arrays of Random Numbers

Julia can create new arrays filled with random numbers. Random numbers generated by the **rand** function are uniformly distributed on the interval 0 to 1:

```
julia> u = rand(Float64,4)       # 4 is the size of the array to be created
4-element Array{Float64,1}:
 0.8532950491539886
 0.1785917912543722
 0.7291637684797312
 0.5697123805250142
```

Julia can also generate normally (Gaussian) distributed random numbers. These random numbers have mean =1.0 and sigma = 1.0

```
julia> u = randn(Float64,4)      # 4 is the size of the array to be created
4-element Array{Float64,1}:
  0.50369094154410528
  0.6354635252942208
  0.6519913327612825
 -0.47638827354968044
```

Create Arrays Using "Collect"

If you need to create a new array and fill it with a range of numbers, the "**collect**" function can be used. "**Collect**" is a function that returns an Array of all items in a collection or iterator. One useful iterator is a range object such as 10:5:25. This iterator represents the numbers from 10 to 25 with a step size of 5. Trying to define an Array using the range object itself doesn't work:

```
julia> a = [10:5:25]             # this doesn't work
1-element Array{StepRange{Int64,Int64},1}:
 10:5:25    # a 1 element array containing the range object
```

It simply returns a 1-element Array containing the range object itself. **Collect** converts the range object into an actual range of numbers:

```
julia> collect(10:5:25)          # creates a new array filled with numbers
4-element Array{Int64,1}:
 10
 15
 20
 25
```

You can use the |> syntax to send the results of the range object to the collect function:

```
julia> (10:5:25) |> collect
4-element Array{Int64,1}:
 10
 15
 20
 25
```

You can specify the Type of elements in the resulting Array:

```
julia> collect(Float64, 10:5:15)
4-element Array{Float64,1}:
 10.0
 15.0
```

Create Arrays Using a Semicolon

As described in the previous section, this doesn't work:

```
julia> a = [10:5:25]
1-element Array{StepRange{Int64,Int64},1}:
 10:5:25
```

Instead of creating an array of numbers, this syntax creates a 1-element array that contain the range object itself - not the range you probably wanted. You can use "collect" to get the array you intended as described, but there is an easier way. Simply end the range object with a semicolon (;):

```
julia> a = [10:5:25;]          # use a semicolon to create an array
4-element Array{Int64,1}:
 10
 15
 20
 25
```

Create Arrays Using Comprehensions

"**Comprehensions**" are another way to create and initialize an Array. A Comprehension consists of an equation with 1 or more variables and a range of values for each of those variables. The resulting Array will have as many dimensions as the number of variables in the equation. For example:

```
julia> a = [(x^2 + 1) for x = 2:5]
4-element Array{Int64,1}:      # a single variable (x) creates a 1-dim array
 5
 10
 17
 26
```

The type of an array created using a comprehension can be defined:

```
julia> a = Float64[(x^2 + 1) for x = 2:5]
4-element Array{Float64,1}:
```

> 5.0
> 10.0
> 17.0
> 26.0

The list of variable values does not have to be defined using a range object. Those values can be listed explicitly:

> julia> a = Float64[(x^2 + 1) for x = [2.0, 2.5, 4.0]]
> 5.0
> 7.25
> 17.0

The number of variables in the comprehension determines the number of dimensions in the resulting Array:

> julia> a = [(x^2 + y^2) for x=2:4, y=4:5]   # 2 variables (x,y) produces
> 3x2 Array{Int64,2}:   # a 2-dim array
> 20 29
> 25 34
> 32 41

Notice that the first variable determines the range of indices for the first dimension (row) of the Array. The range of the second variable determines the range of indices for the second dimension (column) of the resulting Array, and so forth.

Comprehensions can be very handy if you have an array of numbers and want to compute another array based on those numbers.

For example, this statement creates an array of numbers representing angles in degrees and ranging from 0.0° to 90.0° inclusive:

> julia> angle = collect(range(0.0,stop=90.0,length=5))   # angles from 0° to 90°
> 5-element Array{Float64,1}:
> 0.0
> 22.5
> 45.0
> 67.5
> 90.0

The following comprehension computes the sine of the angles in degrees (sind) for each of the angles in the array "angle":

> julia> sinAngle = [**sind**(angle[i]) for i=1:**length**(angle)]
> 5-element Array{Float64,1}:
> 0.0
> 0.38268343236508898
> 0.7071067811865476
> 0.9238795325112867
> 1.0

Removing Items from an Array:

Up until now we have been discussing adding items to an Array. It is also possible to remove items from an array using the **pop!** function. By default, **pop!** removes the last item in an array:

```
julia> a = [10, 20, 30, 40]      # create a new 4-element Array
10
20
30
40                               # "40" is the last item in the Array

julia> pop!(a)                   # pop! removes the last item in the Array
40

julia> a
10                               # array a now contains only 3 items
20
30                               # the last item in the Array is now "30"
```

It is also possible to remove the first item in an array:

```
julia> popfirst!(a)
10

julia> a                         # the array now contains only 2 items
20
30
```

The **pop!** functions remove an item from an array and returns that item for further use in the program. If you just want to delete an item from an array, you can use the **deleleat!** function:

```
julia> deleteat!(a,2)            # delete the item at index 2
1-element Array{Int64,1}:        # the array now contains only a single item
20
```

The **replace!** function replaces items in an existing Array with new values:

```
julia> a = [2,3,4,5]             # the Array used to illustrate replace!
2
3
4
5

julia> replace!(a, 3=>0)         # in Array a, replace 3 with 0
2
0
4
5
```

7.6 - Indexing Arrays:

It is important to note that sanity has finally returned to computer programming. Julia (and Fortran) indexes an array of four numbers 1,2,3,4 not 0,1,2,3 as would be the case with Python and all of the flavors of C. As a result, the first element in any array is element number 1, not element number 0. Trying to access element number 0 will result in an error.

A single element of a 1-dimensional Array is indexed using the syntax [i]
A single element of a 2-dimensional Array is indexed using the syntax [i, j]
A single element of a 3-dimensional Array is indexed using the syntax [i, j, k]

Where: "i = the 1st dimension (Row) index
       "j" = the 2nd dimension (Column) index
       "k" = the 3rd dimension index

And so forth for higher dimensions.

A Word About Ranges:

Range iterators are frequently used to index arrays. Ranges are specified using this syntax: range = start:step:end. For example:

```
julia> r = (2:3:8;)              # a series of numbers starting with 2 and
3-element Array{Int64,1}:        # ending with 8 with a step size of 3
2
5
8
```

Unlike Python, Julia includes the final range element in the list of numbers.

Even though a syntax like **2:3:8** is referred to as a "range", there is a different data **function** also named "range( )".

The range function uses this syntax: **range(start, stop=stop,length=n)**. To avoid confusion the parameters are named. The range function generates a series of "n" equally spaced numbers starting with the first number inside the parentheses (start) and ending with the number named "stop".   Unlike Python, the "stop" value is included in the range.

For example:

```
julia> collect(range(1.0,stop=9.0,length=4))
4-element Array{Float64,1}:
1.0
3.6666666666666665
6.333333333333333
9.0
```

You can find the step size for a range using the **step**() function:

```
julia> step(range(1.0,stop=9.0, length=4))
2.6666666666666665
```

You can use the **range**() function if you know step and length. The **range**() function will compute stop:

```
julia> range(1,step=3,length=4)
1:3:10      # stop = 10
```

You can use the **I>** syntax to send the results of the range() function to the collect function as illustrated here:

```
julia> range(1,step=3,length=4) I> collect
4-element Array{Int64,1}:
  1
  4
  7
 10
```

In this case the results of the **range**() function are integers and could be used as array indices, but the results of the **range**( ) function are not suitable as array indices if they are not integers.

Indexing Examples:

An element in a 1-dimensional array is indexed as A[row] without specifying the column number since a 1-dim array has only one column. For example:

```
julia> A = ["one";"two";"three";"four"]      # semicolons separate rows
4-element Array{String,1}:
 "one"
 "two"
 "three"
 "four"
julia> A[2]                    # index a single value from the array
 "two"

julia> A[end]                  # index the last value in the array
 "four"

julia> A[end-1]                # index the next to last value in the array
 "three"

julia> A[2:4]                  # index a range of values from the array
3-element Array{String,1}:
 "two"
 "three"
 "four"

julia> A[1:2:end]              # index elements 1 to end with step size 2
2-element Array{String,1}:
 "one"
 "three"
```

It is possible to loop through every item in an Array using the "**eachindex**" function. Using the Array A previously defined as an example:

```
julia> for index in eachindex(A); println(A[index]); end
one
two
three
four
```

Colons (:) can be used to indicate the entire range of indices for one or more dimension. Using the Array A previously defined as an example:

```
julia> A[:]    # for a 1-dim Array, [:] produces all of the elements in the Array
4-element Array{String,1}:
 "one"
 "two"
 "three"
 "four"
```

For a 1-dim array, it is not necessary to include the [:]

```
julia> A                # for a 1-dim Array, the colon is not necessary
5-element Array{String,1}:
 "one"
 "two"
 "three"
 "four"
```

The [:] syntax is most useful for multi-dimensional arrays.

Create a 2-dimensional array as an example:

```
julia> m1 = [1 2 3; 4 5 6; 7 8 9]        # semicolons separate rows
3×3 Array{Int64,2}:
 1 2 3
 4 5 6
 7 8 9
```

Index all of the elements in row=2 by using a colon where the index for the column should be. Notice the comma before the colon. Also notice that the elements are returned as a 1-dimensional array

```
julia> m1[2,: ]              # row 2, all columns
3-element Array{Int64,1}:
 4
 5
 6
```

Be aware that the following Julia indices do not work as they do in Python:

```
julia> A[:4]           # this does not yield A[0:4] as it would
 "four"                # in Python

julia> A[4:]           # this yields a syntax error, not A[4:end]
ERROR: syntax: missing last argument in "4:" range expression
```

7.7 - Changing Array Structure

Data arrays are artificial constructs used to make visualizing large amounts of data easier for the programmer. The data structure can be changed without changing the data itself. For example here is a 1-dim array of 16 numbers:

```
julia> a1 = [1 2 3 4 5 6 7 8 9 10 11 12 13 14 15 16]
1×16 Array{Int64,2}:
 1 2 3 4 5 6 7 8 9 10 11 12 13 14 15 16
```

The **reshape**() function can be used to change the visual representation of the data array without changing any of the data. For example:

```
julia> b = reshape(a1,4,4)     # reshape the data in a1 into a 2-dim array
4×4 Array{Int64,2}:            # with 4 rows and 4 columns
 1 5  9 13                     #
 2 6 10 14                     # notice that the data are arranged in column
 3 7 11 15                     # order filling col 1 first then col 2 and ...
 4 8 12 16                     #
```

We can now visualize and index the data as a 2-dim array:

```
julia> b[2,3]                  # the element in row 2 column 3
10
```

But the underlying data is still 1-dimensional and can be indexed as such:

```
julia> b[10]
10
```

Element b[2,3] , b[10], and a1[10] all refer to the same data

```
julia> b[10] == a1[10]== b[2,3]
true
```

We can reshape the same data into a 3-dim array:

```
julia> c = reshape(a1,2,4,2)   # 2 rows, 4 columns and 2 sheets
2×4×2 Array{Int64,3}:
[:, :, 1] =                    # [:,:,1] refers to all of the rows and columns in sheet 1
 1  3  5  7
 2  4  6  8

[:, :, 2] =                    # [:,:,1] refers to all of the rows and columns in sheet 2
  9 11 13 15
 10 12 14 16
```

The data can now be indexed as a 3-dim array:

```
julia> c[2,3,1]                # row 2, col 3, of sheet 2
6
```

And can still be indexed as if it were a 1-dim array:

```
julia> c[6]
6
```

7.8 - Array Functions:

Julia has several elementary functions that operate on arrays. As an example consider the array "b":

```
julia> b = [3;2;4;5]
3
2
4
5

julia> first(b)        # returns the first element in b
3

julia> last(b)         # returns the last element in b
5

julia> length(b)       # returns the number of items in the array
4
```

Note that in Julia length() refers to the number of elements in an array. Generally the "length" of a Vector array is the sqrt of the sum of the squares of the components. This is not that length.

```
julia> typeof(b)       # returns the Type of data the Array contains
Array{Int64,1}

julia> sum(b)          # returns the sum of array items if they are numerical
14

julia> maximum(b)      # returns the maximum element value
5

julia> minimum(b)      # returns the minimum element value
2

julia> c = copy(b)           # makes a copy of b
3
2
4
5

julia> sort(b)         # sorts in ascending order
2
3
4
5
```

The statement **sort**(b) displays a sorted list of the elements of b, but does **not** actually change the array b.

```
julia> b
3                         # array b has not been changed
2
4
5
```

To actually sort the array, you can define a new array containing the sorted elements of the original array:

```
julia> c = sort(b)
2
3
4
5
```

Once again, the array b has not been changed. To sort the original array b in place you must use **sort!**()

```
julia> sort!(b)
2
3
4
5
```

You can also sort in reverse order by specifying the keyword "rev=true"

```
julia> sort(b,rev=true)        # sorts in descending order
5
4
3
2
```

7.9 - Vector Statistics:

Various statistical parameters of a Vector Array can be computed after using the Pkg manager to import the Statistics package as described in Chapter 2:

In the Julia REPL do these steps:

```
julia> ]                        # launches the pkg manager
(v1.0) pkg> add Statistics              # adds the Statistics pkg
(v1.0) pkg> press the "delete" key      # pressing "delete" returns to Julia
julia> using Statistics        # makes Statistics available
```

All of the functions in the Statistics Pkg are now available to be used.

```
julia> b = [2;3;4;5]           # an example array
2
3
4
5
```

```
julia> sum(b)        # returns the sum of all items in array b
14

julia> mean(b)       # returns the mean of items in b
3.5

julia> median(b)
3.5

julia> var(b)        # returns the variance of the items in b
1.6666666666666667

julia> std(b)        # returns the standard deviation of the items in b
1.2909944487358056
```

Julia offers two ways to compute the standard deviation of an array of numbers. Which version is used depends upon the value of a parameter "**corrected**". If corrected=**true**, then the standard deviation sum is divided by n-1 where n = length(Array). If corrected=**false** then the standard deviation sum is divided by n.

```
julia> std(b;corrected=true)  # std with corrected=true (n-1)
1.2909944487358056

julia> std(b;corrected=false) # std with corrected=false (n)
1.11803398874989
```

The default is corrected=**true**.

Julia can compute the correlation between two Vector arrays. For example:

```
julia> b = [2;3;;4;5;6]
julia> d = [4;5;9;9;12]
julia> cor(b,d)
0.9667364890456636
```

7.10 - Vector Arithmetic:

Common arithmetic operations can be applied to arrays. Some examples:

```
julia> a = [2;3;4]              # create a 3 element Array
2
3
4

julia> b = 2* a                 # multiply each element in a by 2
4                               # the '*' in 2*a is optional
6                               # this expression could have been written 2a
8                               # without the *

julia> b/2                      # element by element division
2.0
3.0
4.0
```

70

For some operations, the element by element operation must be stated explicitly using a dot notation.

```
julia> a.+5          # .+ means element by element addition
7
8
9

julia> a.-5          # .- means element by element subtraction
-3
-2
-1
```

All of these arithmetic operators allow a dot notation version for element by element vector computations:

-, +, *, /, \, ^

Element by element exponentiation is performed with this syntax:

```
julia> a = [2;3;4]      # the example Array
2
3
4
julia> b = a.^2         # square each element of Array a
4
9
16
```

Element by element trigonometric functions also require dot notation:

```
julia> angle = [0.0, pi/2, 1.5pi]
0.0
1.5707963267948966
4.71238898038469

julia> sin.(angle)      # notice the dot between sin and (angle)
0.0
1.0
-1.0
```

The log and exp functions also have dot syntax for element by element operation:

```
julia> log.(ones(3))    # notice the dot following log
3-element Array{Float64,1}:
0.0
0.0
0.0
```

String concatenation can be done on an element by element basis:

```
julia> a = [1;2;3]      # example of an Array of numbers
1
2
3
```

```
julia> b = ["one";"two";"three"]          # example of an Array of strings
"one"
"two"
"three"
```

```
julia> string (a,". ",b)   # without dot notation "string" just concatenates a and b
"[1, 2, 3]. [\"one\", \"two\", \"three\"]"
```

```
julia> string. (a,". ",b)        # with dot notation "string." concatenates
"1. one"                         # a and b element by element
"2. two"
"3. three"
```

Element by element comparisons can also be done using the "dot" syntax:

```
julia> a .> 3                    # this statement is: a 'dot'> 3
3-element BitArray{1}:
false
false
 true
```

This would be useful for extracting elements from an array that satisfy some criterion.

7.11 - Array Iteration:

There are two recommended ways to iterate over a whole Array:

```
for a in A
    # do something with the element "a"
end
```

or

```
for i in eachindex(A)
    # do something with index "i" or with element A[i]
end
```

7.12 - Linear Algebra

Define two example arrays:

```
julia> a = [2,3,4]
 2
 3
 4
julia> b = [5,6,7]
 5
 6
 7
```

Julia can do vector addition "out of the box":

```
julia> a+b
 7
 9
 11
```

But, in order to make use of Julia's Linear Algebra functions, it is necessary to "add" the LinearAlgebra pkg. To add the LinearAlgebra pkg from the REPL, start by typing the "right-bracket" character:

```
julia> ]                                # launches the pkg manager
(v1.0) pkg> add LinearAlgebra           # adds the LinearAlgebra pkg
(v1.0) pkg> press the "delete" key      # pressing "delete" returns to Julia
julia> using LinearAlgebra              # makes LinearAlgebra available

julia> dot(a,b)                         # dot product
56

julia> cross(a,b)                       # cross product
3-element Array{Int64,1}:
 -3
  6
 -3
```

Simply multiplying two 1-dimensional arrays yields an error:

```
julia> c = a * b
ERROR: MethodError:
```

One of the vectors must be transposed before vector multiplication is possible. This can be accomplished using the **transpose**() function:

```
julia> c = transpose(a)        # transpose syntax #1
1×3 LinearAlgebra.Transpose{Int64,Array{Int64,1}}:
 2 3 4
```

Transposition can also be accomplished using an apostrophe ('):

```
julia> c = a'                    # transpose syntax #2
1×3 LinearAlgebra.Adjoint{Int64,Array{Int64,1}}:
 2 3 4
```

There are two syntaxes for vector multiplication:

```
julia> d = b * c                 # vector multiplication syntax #1
3×3 Array{Int64,2}:
 10 15 20
 12 18 24
 14 21 28
```

```
julia> d = *(b,c)                # vector multiplication syntax #2
3×3 Array{Int64,2}:
 10 15 20
 12 18 24
 14 21 28
```

```
julia> e = a / b                 # vector division
3×3 Array{Float64,2}:
 0.0909091 0.109091 0.127273
 0.136364  0.163636 0.190909
 0.181818  0.218182 0.254545
```

The Linear Algebra package includes functions for other computations:

```
julia> a = [1 2;3 4]    # create a 2-dim array
2×2 Array{Int64,2}:
 1 2
 3 4
```

```
julia> det(a)
-2.0
```

```
julia> rank(a)
2
```

```
julia> eigvals(a)
2-element Array{Float64,1}:
 -0.3722813232690143
  5.372281323269014
```

Julia can compute a matrix inverse:

```
julia> M = [2 5;1 3]
2×2 Array{Int64,2}:
 2  5
 1  3


julia> N = inv(M)
2×2 Array{Float64,2}:
  3.0  -5.0
 -1.0   2.0


julia> M*N
2×2 Array{Float64,2}:
 1.0  0.0
 0.0  1.0
```

For more details see the Linear Algebra section of the standard library

https://docs.julialang.org/en/v1/stdlib/LinearAlgebra/#stdlib-blas-trans-1

Chapter 8

Data Frames

In the previous chapter we introduced multi dimensional data arrays. In this chapter we will discuss a specific type of data array called a "DataFrame". DataFrames are used in many fields such as statistical analysis of large data sets and machine learning.

A DataFrame is Julia's version of a spreadsheet. This is illustrated by the figure below which shows an actual spreadsheet created using the Macintosh "Numbers" app. It looks better than the Julia representations which we will come to shortly.

Julia DataFrame

Row	Col 1 Name1 Data Type	Col 2 Name2 Data Type	Col 3 Name3 Data Type	Col 4 Name4 Data Type
1				
2				
3				
4				
5				

A DataFrame consists of a 2-dimensional array of data with an additional header row containing (optionally) column numbers, column names, and the Type of data that column contains. In addition there is an extra column pre-pended to the left side of the DataFrame containing row numbers. These row numbers are supplied automatically.

DataFrames provide functionality that simple arrays do not.

- The programmer can refer to columns by name
- There are DataFrame functions that can deal with missing data which is fairly common with real world data sets.
- A DataFrame can have different types of data in different columns. With DataArrays, all columns contain the same data type

Installing "DataFrames" in the Julia REPL:

DataFrame functions are not included as part of the Base Julia installation and must be added using the package manager (pkg). Start by typing a right-square-bracket ( ]) at the julia prompt:

```
julia> ]                          # this launches the pkg manager
(v1.0) pkg> add DataFrames        # add "DataFrames" (plural)
delete                            # press the delete key
julia> using DataFrames           # returns you to the julia prompt
```

You have to finish the installation by typing "using DataFrames" at the Julia prompt. This makes all of the DataFrame functionality available. When you use the pkg manager to add DataFrames, or any package for that matter, Julia goes out to the github repository and downloads the DataFrames package. It then compiles that package, so this whole process may take several minutes depending upon Internet traffic.

Creating DataFrames:

One way to create a new DataFrame is to create an empty DataFrame by defining only the column names and the data Types for each column:

```
julia>emptyDF=DataFrame(Name=String[], Height=Int64[], Weight=Float64[])
0×3 DataFrame          # empty DataFrames are not displayed
```

Remember the square brackets [ ] that define the column data as arrays. Without any data from which Julia can deduce data Types, it is necessary to define the data Type for each column.

Another way to create a new DataFrame is to define the column names and the first row of data all in one expression:

```
julia> dF = DataFrame(Name="Joe", Height=72, Weight=175.0)
1×3 DataFrame
```

This results in a new DataFrame containing one row of data. The Type of the data supplied allows Julia to deduce the data Type for each column.

```
| Row | Name   | Height | Weight  |
|     | String | Int64  | Float64 |
+-----+--------+--------+---------+
| 1   | Joe    | 72     | 175.0   |
```

This method can be expanded to define more than one row of data. Notice that each row of data is a row array –> the elements are separated by semicolons:

```
julia> df = DataFrame(Name=["Jim";"Joe"],
                      Height=[65;70],
                      Weight=[156.5;170.8])
2×3 DataFrame
```

```
julia> df
```

| Row | Name | Height | Weight |
	String	Int64	Float64
1	Jim	65	156.5
2	Joe	70	170.8

Adding Rows Using Concatenation

At this point we have a DataFrame, **df**, with column names and data Types defined and two rows of data as illustrated. One way to add rows of data is to define a new DataFrame with one or more rows of data as illustrated below.

Here is a new DataFrame with one instance of new data:

```
julia> newDF = DataFrame(Name=["Tom"],Height=[67],Weight=[158.3])
1×3 DataFrame
```

| Row | Name | Height | Weight |
	String	Int64	Float64
1	Tom	67	158.3

We can now concatenate the old (**df**) and new (**newDF**) DataFrames using the concatenation function **vcat**() which concatenates in the vertical direction.

```
julia> vcat(df, newDF)        # concatenate the old and new data
3×3 DataFrame
```

We now have a new version of df containing 3 instances (rows) of data:

| Row | Name | Height | Weight |
	String	Int64	Float64
1	Jim	65	156.5
2	Joe	70	170.8
3	Tom	67	158.3

It is possible to continue adding one or more rows of data to the DataFrame using **vcat**(). This is particularly handy if you have multiple sources of data that you want to combine into a single DataFrame.

Adding Rows Using push!()

You can also add rows of data to an existing DataFrame using the function **push!()**. To use **push!()**, you create a row vector containing the new data. There is no need to create a new DataFrame.

```
julia> newData = ["Bill" 62 135.6]        # data elements separated by spaces
1×3 Array{Any,2}:
 "Bill"  62  135.6

julia> push!(df, newData)
4×3 DataFrame
```

| Row | Name | Height | Weight |
	String	Int64	Float64
1	Jim	65	156.5
2	Joe	70	170.8
3	Tom	67	158.3
4	Bill	62	135.6

It is possible to **push!()** several rows of data onto the end of an existing DataFrame but you have to do it one row at a time. Here is a 3x3 data Array containing 2 rows of new data:

```
julia> newData = ["Tim" 71 180.0; "Bob" 63 132.5]
2×3 Array{Any,2}:

 "Tim"  71  180.0
 "Bob"  63  132.5
```

A simple loop can then be used to **push!()** each row of the array onto the end of the df DataFrame:

```
julia> for row in 1:2
            push!(df, newData[row,:])
        end
```

We now have a DataFrame with 6 rows of data and an easy way to add more rows.

```
julia> df
6×3 DataFrame
```

| Row | Name | Height | Weight |
	String	Int64	Float64
1	Jim	65	156.5
2	Joe	70	170.8
3	Tom	67	158.3
4	Bill	62	135.6
5	Tim	71	180.0
6	Bob	63	132.5

Adding Rows Using append!()

It is also possible to use the **append!**() function to combine DataFrames and thereby add multiple rows of new data to an existing DataFrame. For example, we have the 6 row DataFrame, **df** ,from the previous example. If we have a separate DataFrame containing some new data, we can combine the original and the new DataFrame using **append!**().

Define a new DataFrame, **df2**, containing new data:

```
julia> df2 = DataFrame(Name   = ["Pim";"Zoe"],
                       Height = [65;70],
                       Weight = [156.5;170.8])
```

| Row | Name | Height | Weight |
	String	Int64	Float64
1	Pim	65	156.5
2	Zoe	70	170.8

Combine the two DataFrames using the **append!**() function:

```
julia> append!(df,df2)
```

| Row | Name | Height | Weight |
	String	Int64	Float64
1	Jim	65	156.5
2	Joe	70	170.8
3	Tom	67	158.3
4	Bill	62	135.6
5	Tim	71	180.0
6	Bob	63	132.5
7	Pim	65	156.5
8	Zoe	70	170.8

Deleting Rows

Deleting rows can be done using the **deleterows!**() function:

```
julia> deleterows!(df, 4:8)     # 4:8 specifies the range of rows to delete
```

| Row | Name | Height | Weight |
	String	Int64	Float64
1	Jim	65	156.5
2	Joe	70	170.8
3	Tom	67	158.3

Adding Columns

A new column of data can be added to the right end of an existing DataFrame using this syntax:

```
julia> df[:Age] = [25, 32, 18]     # :Age is a new name
3-element Array{Int64,1}:
 25
 32
 18
```

In the statement df[:**Age**], "**Age**" will be the name of the new column and the column array of data [25; 32; 18] will be the contents of the new column. The number of elements in this data array must match the number of rows in the exiting DataFrame.

```
julia> df
3×4 DataFrame
| Row | Name   | Height | Weight  | Age   |
|     | String | Int64  | Float64 | Int64 |
+-----+--------+--------+---------+-------+
| 1   | Jim    | 65     | 156.5   | 25    |
| 2   | Joe    | 70     | 170.8   | 32    |
| 3   | Tom    | 67     | 158.3   | 18    |
```

Adding Computed Columns

It is possible to add a column containing data computed using data from other existing columns. For example to add a new column containing BMI (Body Mass Index) computed from Height and Weight use this syntax:

```
julia> df[:BMI] =
       map((x,y)->705.0*x/y^2,df[:Weight],df[:Height])
```

The expression, **(x,y)->705.0*x/y^2** is the equation to compute BMI where x = Weight (lb) and y = Height (inches). When evaluating this expression, the column :Weight is used as the variable "x" and the column :Height is used as the 'y' variable. The net effect of this statement is to add a new column and give it the name "BMI" and then to fill that new column with values computed using the Height and Weight data already in the DataFrame.

```
julia> dF
3×5 DataFrame
| Row | Name   | Height | Weight  | Age   | BMI     |
|     | String | Int64  | Float64 | Int64 | Float64 |
+-----+--------+--------+---------+-------+---------+
| 1   | Jim    | 65     | 156.5   | 25    | 26.1142 |
| 2   | Joe    | 70     | 170.8   | 32    | 24.5743 |
| 3   | Tom    | 67     | 158.3   | 18    | 24.8611 |
```

Renaming Columns

An existing column name can be changed using the **rename!**() function. To change the name of the first column of df from "**Name**" to "**User**" use this syntax:

```
julia> rename!(df, :Name => :User)
| Row | User   | Height | Weight  | Age   | BMI     |
|     | String | Int64  | Float64 | Int64 | Float64 |
|-----|--------|--------|---------|-------|---------|
| 1   | Jim    | 65     | 156.5   | 25    | 26.1142 |
| 2   | Joe    | 70     | 170.8   | 32    | 24.5743 |
| 3   | Tom    | 67     | 158.3   | 18    | 24.8611 |
```

Deleting Columns

An existing colum can be deleted using the **delete!**() function. For example to delete the column named "**Age**" do this:

```
julia> delete!(dF, :Age)
| Row | User   | Height | Weight  | BMI     |
|     | String | Int64  | Float64 | Float64 |
|-----|--------|--------|---------|---------|
| 1   | Jim    | 65     | 156.5   | 26.1142 |
| 2   | Joe    | 70     | 170.8   | 24.5743 |
| 3   | Tom    | 67     | 158.3   | 24.8611 |
```

Accessing Data in a DataFrame:

Data in a DataFrame can be accessed using the index numbers for the row and column of the desired data element. I will use the variables row and col rather than the numbers themselves to emphasize which is which.

```
julia> row=2; col=3; dF[row,col]
170.8
```

The colon (:) can be used to signify "all of the elements in". For example to retrieve all of the elements in row 2:

```
julia> dF[row,:]
1×4 DataFrame
| Row | User   | Height | Weight  | BMI     |
|     | String | Int64  | Float64 | Float64 |
|-----|--------|--------|---------|---------|
| 1   | Joe    | 70     | 170.8   | 24.5743 |
```

Notice that even though this is the second row from the dF DataFrame, it is row number "1" in the resulting DataFrame.

To get all of the elements in a column, use the column number:

```
julia> dF[col]          # get all elements in column 3

156.5
170.8
158.3
```

The syntax dF[:,col] using a colon to signify "all rows" still works in Julia v1.0, but it generates a warning and should be avoided in the future.

It is also possible to index columns in a DataFrame using the column name preceded by a colon:

```
julia> dF[:Weight]

156.5
170.8
158.3
```

You can retrieve all rows from multiple columns in a single statement using column names:

```
julia> dF[[:Weight, :BMI]]    # note the double brackets

| Row | Weight  | BMI     |
|     | Float64 | Float64 |
├─────┼─────────┼─────────┤
| 1   | 156.5   | 26.1142 |
| 2   | 170.8   | 24.5743 |
| 3   | 158.3   | 24.8611 |
```

Or, using column numbers:

```
julia> dF[[3,4]]              # note the double brackets

| Row | Weight  | BMI     |
|     | Float64 | Float64 |
├─────┼─────────┼─────────┤
| 1   | 156.5   | 26.1142 |
| 2   | 170.8   | 24.5743 |
| 3   | 158.3   | 24.8611 |
```

This latter syntax is handy if you need to access columns based on variable values:

```
julia> a=3; b=4 ; dF[[a,b]]

| Row | Weight  | BMI     |
|     | Float64 | Float64 |
├─────┼─────────┼─────────┤
| 1   | 156.5   | 26.1142 |
| 2   | 170.8   | 24.5743 |
| 3   | 158.3   | 24.8611 |
```

A range of rows and columns can be accessed in a single expression to retrieve a rectangular portion of the DataFrame:

```
julia> r1=2; r2=3; c1=3; c2=4; dF[r1:r2, [c1,c2]]

| Row | Weight  | BMI     |
|     | Float64 | Float64 |
├─────┼─────────┼─────────┤
| 1   | 170.8   | 24.5743 |
| 2   | 158.3   | 24.8611 |
```

The selection of rows and columns do not have to be contiguous. You can specify specific rows and columns using row and column numbers or names:

```
julia> dF[[1,3], [1,4]]

| Row | User   | BMI     |
|     | String | Float64 |
├─────┼────────┼─────────┤
| 1   | Jim    | 26.1142 |
| 2   | Tom    | 24.8611 |
```

You can access all rows from specific columns using this syntax:

```
julia> dF[[1,4]]
3×2 DataFrame
| Row | User   | BMI     |
|     | String | Float64 |
├─────┼────────┼─────────┤
| 1   | Jim    | 26.1142 |
| 2   | Joe    | 24.5743 |
| 3   | Tom    | 24.8611 |
```

Conditional Selections

You can select a portion of a DataFrame based on conditional testing of the values in that DataFrame. For example, to select only rows from dF where the Height (Column 2) is greater than 65:

```
julia> dF[dF[:2] .> 65, :]

| Row | User   | Height | Weight  | BMI     |
|     | String | Int64  | Float64 | Float64 |
├─────┼────────┼────────┼─────────┼─────────┤
| 1   | Joe    | 70     | 170.8   | 24.5743 |
| 2   | Tom    | 67     | 158.3   | 24.8611 |
```

Note that Jim has been eliminated from the resulting DataFrame.

DataFrame Functions

There are several functions that operate on DataFrames or on the data they contain

Column Statistics

There are many statistics functions that can be applied to DataFrame data, but the Statistics package is not part of the standard Julia installation. To make use of these Statistical functions, you must first add the Statistics package (pkg) to your REPL or code file. From the Julia prompt in the REPL, type a right bracket]. This will launch the package manager pkg:

```
julia> ]                         # type a right bracket ]
(v1.0) pkg> add Statistics       # enter add Statistics
        •
        •                        # a long delay while Statistics is being compiled
        •
(v1.0) pkg> delete               # press the delete key
julia> using Statistics          # at the Julia prompt type using Statistics
```

mean, median, maximum, minimum, standard deviation

You can now compute these statistics for a column of data. You can identify the column to be used by Name or by column number:

```
julia> mean(dF[:Weight])      # column identified by Name
161.86666666666667


julia> mean(dF[:3])           # column identified by number
161.86666666666667


julia> median(dF[:Weight])
158.3


julia> maximum(dF[:Weight])
170.8


julia> minimum(dF[:Weight])
156.5


julia> std(dF[:Weight])       # standard deviation
7.7886669805129936
```

Correlation Between Columns

The Pearson correlation coefficient between two columns of a DataFrame can be found using the **cor**() function. Using the DataFrame dF2 as an example:

```
| Row | Height | Weight  | BMI     |
|     | Int64  | Float64 | Float64 |
|-----|--------|---------|---------|
| 1   | 65     | 156.5   | 26.1142 |
| 2   | 70     | 170.8   | 24.5743 |
| 3   | 67     | 158.3   | 24.8611 |

julia> cor(dF2[:Weight],dF2[:BMI])
-0.7280248354430096

julia> cor(dF2[:Height],dF2[:BMI])
-0.8949249711229895
```

The negative correlation between BMI and Height is reasonable - as Height goes up, BMI goes down. But the negative correlation between Weight and BMI is suspicious. I basically picked these numbers out of the air and apparently did not do a very realistic job of it.

eachcol()

In the previous section we applied statistical functions to individual columns of data. It is also possible to operate on each column of data by using the **eachcol**() function.

```
julia> for col in eachcol(dF2)
           println(col)
       end
(:Height, [65, 70, 67])
(:Weight, [156.5, 170.8, 158.3])
(:BMI, [26.1142, 24.5743, 24.8611])
```

The eachcol() function returns a tuple for each column in the DataFrame. This tuple contains two elements:

1. The name of the column as col[1], and
2. The data contents of the column as an array of data col[2].

```
julia> for col in eachcol(dF2)
           println(col[1])
       end
Height
Weight
BMI
```

```
julia> for col in eachcol(dF2)
           println(col[2])
       end
[65, 70, 67]
[156.5, 170.8, 158.3]
[26.1142, 24.5743, 24.8611]
```

So, it is possible to compute a statistic for every column using a single statement:

```
julia> for col in eachcol(dF2)
           println(mean(col[2]))
       end
67.33333333333333
161.86666666666667
25.183197273621044
```

The **eachcol**() function would be useful if you wanted to export just the data in a DataFrame without the fancy decorations and column names.

eachrow()

Just as there is an eachcol() function, so also is there an **eachrow**() function. Using the dF2 DataFrame as example, the **eachrow**() function returns the following:

```
julia> for row in eachrow(dF2)
           println(row)
       end

DataFrameRow (row 1)
Height   65
Weight   156.5
BMI      26.114201183431952

DataFrameRow (row 2)
Height   70
Weight   170.8
BMI      24.57428571428572

DataFrameRow (row 3)
Height   67
Weight   158.3
BMI      24.86110492314547
```

It is possible to export just the data from a DataFrame using the **eachrow()** function:

```
julia> for row in eachrow(dF2)
            println(row[1]," ",row[2]," ",row[3])
       end
65  156.5  26.114201183431952
70  170.8  24.57428571428572
67  158.3  24.86110492314547
```

Miscellaneous DataFrame Functions

describe()

The **describe()** function provides a summary of the contents of the specified DataFrame. For example applying **describe()** to the DataFrame **dF** results in this very wide summary.

```
julia> describe(dF)
```

Row	variable Symbol	mean Union...	min Any	median Union...	max Any	nunique Union...	nmissing Nothing	eltype DataType
1	User		Jim		Tom	3		String
2	Height	67.3333	65	67.0	70			Int64
3	Weight	161.867	156.5	158.3	170.8			Float64
4	BMI	25.1832	24.5743	24.8611	26.1142			Float64

First, recognize that this "description" is itself a DataFrame, so the Row numbers apply to this DataFrame and not to the DataFrame, dF, being "described". The contents of this DataFrame are a description of and some statistics about the columns in the dF DataFrame. The columns in this description contain the names of the columns in dF along with the mean, min, median, and max values of the dF column contents. "nunique" is the number of unique entries in the column - in this case there are 3 unique Users: Jim, Joe, and Tom. The "eltype" column indicates that the data Types of each column's contents.

The "missing" column indicates that, in this case, there are no missing data elements in any of the columns. Missing data will be discussed in the next section.

names()

The **names()** function returns the column names from a DataFrame:

```
julia> names(dF2)
3-element Array{Symbol,1}:
 :Height
 :Weight
 :BMI
```

sort!()

The **sort!**() function allows sorting of the rows in a DataFrame. Using the DataFrame df as an example:

```
julia> df          # this is the unsorted DataFrame

| Row | Name   | Height | Weight  |
|     | String | Int64  | Float64 |
|-----+--------+--------+---------|
| 1   | Jim    | 65     | 156.5   |
| 2   | Tom    | 67     | 158.3   |
| 3   | Joe    | 70     | 170.8   |
| 4   | Bill   | 62     | 135.6   |
| 5   | Pim    | 58     | 170.8   |
| 6   | Zoe    | 67     | 155.6   |
```

The following **sort!**() statement sorts the DataFrame df rows in ascending order of Height and then Weight if there are more than one row with the same Height:

```
julia> sort!(df,[order(:Height), order(:Weight)])

| Row | Name   | Height | Weight  |
|     | String | Int64  | Float64 |
|-----+--------+--------+---------|
| 1   | Pim    | 58     | 170.8   |
| 2   | Bill   | 62     | 135.6   |
| 3   | Jim    | 65     | 156.5   |
| 4   | Zoe    | 67     | 155.6   |
| 5   | Tom    | 67     | 158.3   |
| 6   | Joe    | 70     | 170.8   |
```

Sort!() can also sort alphabetically if some columns contain String data:

```
julia> sort!(df,[order(:Name)])

| Row | Name   | Height | Weight  |
|     | String | Int64  | Float64 |
|-----+--------+--------+---------|
| 1   | Bill   | 62     | 135.6   |
| 2   | Jim    | 65     | 156.5   |
| 3   | Joe    | 70     | 170.8   |
| 4   | Pim    | 58     | 170.8   |
| 5   | Tom    | 67     | 158.3   |
| 6   | Zoe    | 67     | 155.6   |
```

Sort!() can also sort in reverse order by using the "rev=true" parameter:

```
julia> sort!(df,[order(:Name)], rev=true)

| Row | Name   | Height | Weight  |
|     | String | Int64  | Float64 |
+-----+--------+--------+---------+
| 1   | Zoe    | 67     | 155.6   |
| 2   | Tom    | 67     | 158.3   |
| 3   | Pim    | 58     | 170.8   |
| 4   | Joe    | 70     | 170.8   |
| 5   | Jim    | 65     | 156.5   |
| 6   | Bill   | 62     | 135.6   |
```

head() and tail()

For very long DataFrames, the **head**() function can be used to list the first few lines and **tail**() can be used to list the last few lines. Here is an example from a DataFrame with only 9 rows of data:

```
julia> head(dfTest2)

| Row | UserID  | Height | Weight  |
|     | String⬚ | Int64⬚ | Int64⬚  |
+-----+---------+--------+---------+
| 1   | User01  | 65     | 155     |
| 2   | User02  | 71     | 191     |
| 3   | User03  | 62     | 172     |
| 4   | User04  | 68     | 163     |
| 5   | User05  | 72     | 205     |
| 6   | User06  | 61     | missing |
```

```
julia> tail(dfTest2)

| Row | UserID  | Height  | Weight  |
|     | String⬚ | Int64⬚  | Int64⬚  |
+-----+---------+---------+---------+
| 1   | User04  | 68      | 163     |
| 2   | User05  | 72      | 205     |
| 3   | User06  | 61      | missing |
| 4   | User07  | 65      | 156     |
| 5   | User08  | missing | 183     |
| 6   | User09  | 67      | 168     |
```

Importing a DataFrame from a CSV File

In order to read delimited files, for example a comma separated file (csv), it is necessary to add the package (pkg) CSV.

julia>]	# type a right bracket]
(v1.0) pkg> **add CSV**	# type add CSV
•	
•	# a long delay while CSV is being compiled
•	
(v1.0) pkg> delete	# press the delete key to return to Julia
julia> **using CSV**	# at the Julia prompt type using CSV

To demonstrate importing a CSV file, I started by creating a spreadsheet using Mac "Numbers" as illustrated below:

Header Row ➡

UserID	Height	Weight
User01	65	155
User02	71	191
User03	62	172
User04	68	163
User05	72	205
User06	61	
User07	65	156
User08		183
User09	67	168

This spreadsheet has one header row containing the names of the columns followed by nine rows of data. Notice that there are two data cells shown outlined that do not contain data -- the data for these cells is "missing". Missing data is a common problem for real world data sets. In addition to data that is simply missing, there may be other data that are clearly wrong. They may be wrong because they are "outliers" -- values that are so far from the rest of the data that they are clearly wrong. Or perhaps there was a data "glitch" causing the wrong data to be entered. Whatever the reason, Julia DataFrames has functions to handle missing data.

This spreadsheet of data was exported to a CSV file shown here:

UserID,Height,Weight	# the header row
User01,65,155	
User02,71,191	
User03,62,172	
User04,68,163	
User05,72,205	
User06,61,	# missing data
User07,65,156	
User08,,183	# missing data (,,)
User09,67,168	

The missing data in the User06 row is simply not there. The missing data in the User08 row is identified by two consecutive commas.

The Julia CSV package has the ability to read a CSV file and convert it into a DataFrame all in a single statement:

```
julia> dfTest2 = CSV.File("CSV_File.csv") |> DataFrame

| Row | UserID  | Height  | Weight  |
|     | String␣ | Int64␣  | Int64␣  |
|-----|---------|---------|---------|
| 1   | User01  | 65      | 155     |
| 2   | User02  | 71      | 191     |
| 3   | User03  | 62      | 172     |
| 4   | User04  | 68      | 163     |
| 5   | User05  | 72      | 205     |
| 6   | User06  | 61      | missing |
| 7   | User07  | 65      | 156     |
| 8   | User08  | missing | 183     |
| 9   | User09  | 67      | 168     |
```

The CSV.File() function has correctly identified the header row and the data rows. Notice that the missing data in rows 6 and 8 has been correctly identified as **missing**. In this case 'missing' is not a String -- it is an instance of a new data Type **Missing**. In fact it is the only instance of that data Type. DataFrame functions have the capability to identify and to ignore data identified as **missing**. This will be discussed later.

But first, we need to talk a little more about the **CSV.File()** function. There are several keyword arguments that can be included in the call to **CSV.File()**. None are shown in the example above because all of the default values for these arguments work fine for this particular CSV file. In order to include keyword arguments in the CSV.File() function call, insert a semicolon followed by a list of comma separated keyword arguments. An example will be given after we discuss some of the available keyword arguments.

```
julia> df = CSV.File("CSV_File.csv"; keyword args) |> DataFrame
```

CSV.File Keyword Arguments

There are many keyword arguments and only a subset will be discussed here. For a full discussion refer to the CSV.File site:

https://juliadata.github.io/CSV.jl/stable/index.html#CSV.File

File Layout Options:

header=n: where n can be an Int or a Range of Ints, indicating a span of rows to be combined together as column names. Default n=1.

skipto=n: specifies the number of rows to skip before starting to read data. Default=0

footerskip=n: specifies the number of rows at the end of a file to skip. Default=0

Parsing Options:

missingstrings, missingstring: By default, only two consecutive delimiters (,,) is considered missing. This argument can be either a String, or Vector{String} that will be parsed as missing. For example, some data bases use the strings "NA" or "N/A" to signify missing data.

delim=',': a Char that indicates how columns are delimited in a file. A comma is the default. If the source file is tab delimited, use delim='\t' .

decimal='.' a Char that indicates how decimals are separated in floats, For example a period is used in the US: 3.14, and a comma is used in Europe 3,14. The default is period.

truestrings, falsestrings: Vectors of Strings that indicate how true or false values are represented.

Column Type Options:

types: a Vector or Dict of types to be used for column types.

For example:

- Dict(1=>Float64) will set the first column as a Float64,
- Dict(:column1=>Float64) will set the column named column1 to Float64 and,
- Dict("column1"=>Float64) will set the column named column1 to Float64

allowmissing=:all: indicate how missing values are allowed in columns; possible values are:

- :all - all columns may contain missings (the default),
- :auto - auto-detect columns that contain missings or,
- :none - no columns may contain missings

You can use allowmissing=:none and try to read the file. If there are missing values you will get an error alerting you that there are missing values:

ERROR: ArgumentError: `allowmissing=:none`, but missing values were detected in csv file

Here is an example using the keyword arguments **skipto** and **footerskip**:

```
julia> dfTest3 = CSV.File("CSV_File.csv";
                skipto=5, footerskip=3) |> DataFrame
```

| Row | UserID | Height | Weight |
	String◌	Int64◌	Int64◌
1	User04	68	163
2	User05	72	205
3	User06	61	missing

CSV.File has used row 1 as the header row and has then skipped to row 5 starting at the header row - row 1. The last 3 rows have also been skipped because of the footerskip=3 keyword.

Missing Data

Missing data is common in any DataFrame based on real world measurements. This raises two problems:

1. How to identify the missing data
2. How to avoid using missing data when doing column math.

How to Identify Missing Data:

The **CSV.File**() function has powerful methods for identifying some common missing data forms. By default it identifies two consecutive separator characters (usually commas), or a separator without any following data as instances of missing data.

By using the keyword arguments **missingstrings** and **missingstring** other common ways of identifying missing data can be specified. For example, some data sets use the strings "NA" or "N/A" to signify missing data and CSV.File can be instructed to search for these missing data markers.

In some cases the data is there but it is obviously not correct. A negative weight for example. Or an outlier that is so far from the mean value that it is probably erroneous. CSV.File cannot find these instances for you. In the worst case scenario, you may have to go through your data set and correct or identify missing data yourself.

Regardless of how the missing data is found, it must be identified using the symbol missing. This "missing" is not a string. It is a symbol of Type Missing:

```
julia> typeof(missing)
Missing
```

How to Avoid Using Missing Data:

If you attempt to do a mathematical operation on a column of data with some missing data in it, you will get an error:

```
julia> mean(dfTest2[:Height])
missing
```

Julia provides the function **skipmissing**() to allow mathematical operations to proceed ignoring any missing data:

```
julia> mean(skipmissing(dfTest2[:Height]))
66.375
```

Chapter 9

Other Data Structures

Julia provides support for numerous different data types other than data Arrays and DataFrames.

9.1 - Dictionaries:

A dictionary is an array of data items arranged in a key => value pattern. The => operator is a symbol for the Pair() function. Dictionary items are accessed by giving the key and the dictionary returns the value associated with that key. Keys must be unique – you can't have two keys with the same name in the same dictionary.

A dictionary is defined using the **Dict**() function. For example, this statement defines a dictionary named "members" with the first entry "Joe" identified by the key "name1":

```
julia> members = Dict("name1"=>"Joe")
Dict{String,String} with 1 entry:
  "name1" => "Joe"
```

Additional dictionary entries can be added using the **push!**() function that we have encountered previously.

```
julia> push!(members, "name2"=>"Sam")
Dict{String,String} with 2 entries:
  "name2" => "Sam"
  "name1" => "Joe"
```

Or, even easier, new entries can be added by giving a new key=>value pair:

```
julia> members["name3"] = "Bill"
"Bill"
```

This syntax can be used to change the value assigned to one of the existing keys:

```
julia> members["name3"] = "Bob"
"Bob"

julia> members
  "name2" => "Sam"
  "name3" => "Bob"
  "name1" => "Joe"
```

Dictionary contents can be listed by entering the dictionary name:

> julia> **members**
> "name2" => "Sam"
> "name3" => "Bill"
> "name1" => "Joe"

Individual dictionary entries are accessed by giving the key inside square brackets:

> julia> **members**["name1"]
> "Joe"

Notice the similarity to accessing items in an array by giving the array index inside square brackets. Dictionary items must be indexed by key. Giving an index doesn't work:

> julia> members[2]
> ERROR: KeyError: key 2 not found

It is possible to use integers as keys:

> julia> numbers = Dict(1=>"one")
> julia> numbers[2] = "Two"

> julia> numbers
> 2 => "Two"
> 1 => "one"

> julia> numbers[1]
> "One"

In this case the dictionary items appear to be addressed by index, but the integers are really keys. The second entry could have the key 546. If you want to address entries by index, use an array instead of a dictionary.

The **get**() function can be used to retrieve a value from a dictionary. The advantage of using **get**() is that it provides a default value if the requested key doesn't exist in the dictionary.

We have the members dictionary with three entries:

> julia> members
> "name2" => "Sam"
> "name3" => "Bob"
> "name1" => "Joe"

Retrieve the value associated with the key "name1":

> julia> members["name1"]
> "Joe"

Try to retrieve an entry with the key "name4":

> julia> members["name4"]
> **ERROR**: KeyError: key "name4" not found

Using **get**() allows you to specify a default value to return if the desired key does not exist in th dictionary. In this case the default value is "no such member".

> julia> **get**(members,"name4","**no such member**")
> "no such member"

To see if a dictionary contains a key, use **haskey**():

> julia> **haskey**(members,"name1")
> **true**

> julia> **haskey**(members,"name5")
> **false**

You can list all the keys in a dictionary using the **keys**() function:

> julia> **keys**(members)
> "name1"
> "name2"
> "name3"

Similarly, you can list all of the values in a dictionary using the **values**() function:

> julia> **values**(members)
> "Joe"
> "Sam"
> "Bob"

Or you can list all of the key=>value pairs by simply giving the name of the dictionary:

> julia> **members**
> "name2" => "Sam"
> "name3" => "Bob"
> "name1" => "Joe"

You can delete a key=>value pair from a dictionary, using **delete!**() - notice the exclamation point (**!**):

> julia> members
> Dict{String,String} with **3** entries:
> "name2" => "Sam"
> "name3" => "Bob"
> "name1" => "Tom"

> julia> **delete!**(members, "name1")
> Dict{String,String} with **2** entries:
> "name2" => "Sam"
> "name3" => "Bob"

To iterate through all of the key=>value pairs in a dictionary you can use this syntax:

```
julia> for (key,value) in members
         println(key, " => ", value)
       end

name2 => Sam
name3 => Bob
name1 => Joe
```

You have probably noticed that dictionary entries do not appear in sorted order. You can iterate through a dictionary in sorted order, sorted on keys, by using this syntax:

```
julia> for key in sort(collect(keys(members)))
         println("$key => $(members[key])")
       end

name1 => Joe
name2 => Sam
name3 => Bob
name4 => Tom
```

You can also iterate through values in sorted order:

```
julia> for value in sort(collect(values(members)))
         println("$value")
       end
Bob
Joe
Sam
Tom
```

Julia also provides a sorted dictionary type but that type resides in a package called DataStructures that you must add using the Julia package (pkg) manager.

```
julia> ]                             # start the pkg manager by typing ]
(v1.0) pkg> add DataStructures       # add the DataStructures pkg
julia> using DataStructures          # make DataStructures available
```

The SortedDict type is now available. It works in the same way as a regulat Dict except that the entries are always in sorted order (sorted on keys):

```
julia> sorted_dict = SortedDict("b"=>2, "d"=>5, "a"=>1)
"a" => 1
"b" => 2
"d" => 5
```

Note that the listing of the sorted dictionary is in sorted order even though the entries were not entered in sorted order.

You can add a new key=>value pair just as with an unsorted dictionary:

```
julia> sorted_dict["c"] = 3
3
```

```
julia> sorted_dict
  "a" => 1
  "b" => 2
  "c" => 3
  "d" => 5
```

Suppose you need a dictionary that has several values associated with a single key? This can be accomplished by making the value a named tuple.

```
julia> d3 = Dict("member1" => (name="Frank",age=25,weight=175.0))
  "member1" => (name = "Frank", age = 25, weight = 175.0)
```

In this example, the dictionary d3 contains a key "member1" and a named tuple of three values associated with that member.

```
julia> d3["member1"]
(name = "Frank", age = 25, weight = 175.0)
```

The separate values associated with the key "member1" can be accessed using dot notation:

```
julia> d3["member1"].name    # get the name associated with member1
"Frank"

julia> d3["member1"].age     # get the age associated with member1
25
```

9.2 - The Structure Type

Functionality similar to that just described for dictionaries can be accomplished by defining a new data Type that is a structure:

```
julia> struct Member          # use the key word "struct"
         name::String
         age::Int64
         weight::Float64
       end
```

This statement defines a new data Type named "Member". The Type "Member" has three components: "name" which is a String, "age" which is an Int64, and "weight" which is a Float64. Variables of Type Member can be created using this syntax:

```
julia> m1 = Member("Joe",25,175)
Member("Joe", 25, 175.0)

julia> typeof(m1)      # variable m1 has Type = Member
Member
```

Additional instances of Type Member can be created using the same syntax

```
julia> m2 = Member("Jim",50,225)
```

```
julia> m1.name         # individual components of m1 can be obtained
"Joe"                  # using dot notation

julia> m2.weight
225.0
```

The names of fields in a structure can be listed using the **fieldnames**() function:

```
julia> fieldnames(Member)
(:name, :age, :weight)
```

The colons preceding each fieldname indicates that these are Symbols and not strings.

A data structure of Type Member is immutable. This means that once the field values have been entered, they cannot be changed. An attempt to change one of these values will throw an Error:

```
julia> m2.weight = 245.0
ERROR: type Member is immutable
```

If you need a mutable data structure, that is one where the field values can be changed, then you will need a "mutable struct" as illustrated here:

```
julia> mutable struct MMember         # Type MMember is mutable
          name::String
          age::Int64
          weight::Float64
       end
```

The definition of a mutable struct is the same as for an immutable struct except for the word "mutable". Instances of Type mutable struct can be created using the same syntax as for an immutable struct:

```
julia> mm1 = MMember("Joe",25,175)
julia> mm2 = MMember("Jim",50,225)
```

Individual data fields can be accessed using dot notation as before:

```
julia> mm1.name
"Joe"
```

Because the struct MMember is mutable, it is possible to change the value of field contents. For example, this statement changes the "name" field of mm1 from "Joe" to "Frank":

```
julia> mm1.name = "Frank"
"Frank"
```

9.3 - Other Data Structures:

The Julia package "DataStructures" provides many different types of data structures. We have previously discussed the sorted dictionary structure provided as part of the "Data Structures" package and how to download and install that package using the Julia package manager (pkg).

The DataStructures package implements a variety of data structures, including:

Deque (implemented with an unrolled linked list)
CircularBuffer
CircularDeque
Stack
Queue
Accumulators and Counters
Disjoint Sets
Binary Heap
Mutable Binary Heap
Ordered Dicts and Sets
Dictionaries with Defaults
Trie
Linked List
Sorted Dict, Sorted Multi-Dict and Sorted Set
DataStructures.IntSet
Priority Queue

You can read the documentation for any of these structures at:

http://juliacollections.github.io/DataStructures.jl/latest/

Chapter 10

Flow Control

Computer statements are typically executed in sequential order. A statement is executed and then the next statement is executed and so on. But it is not possible to write useful code based entirely on sequential execution. All modern languages, including Julia, provide ways to implement non-sequential execution.

10.1 - Unconditional Branching

Julia provides two macros to implement unconditional branching in code execution. These are:

@**goto** name_of_label, and
@**label** name_of_label

When the @**goto** name_of_label macro is encountered, it causes an unconditional branch to the statement containing the macro @**label** name_of_label where name_ of_label can be any character or string without quotation marks.

```
julia> function jump(a,b)
          print(a)
       @goto partb
          println("This Statement is Never Executed")
       @label partb
          println(b)
       end

julia> jump("Hello ", "World")
Hello World
```

Julia limits the capability of @goto. The @goto and @label statements must be in the same code block. You cannot @goto a label in a different code block. You cannot @goto an @label at the global level.

The use of unconditional branching is frowned upon since it can lead to "spaghetti code" that is difficult to maintain.

10.2 - Conditional Branching

Conditional branching is implemented in Julia by **if-elseif-else-end** blocks of code.

```
julia> x=5
julia> if(x > 10)
           println("$x > 10")
       elseif(x < 10)          # because 5 is <10
           println("$x < 10")  # this statement gets executed
       else
           println("$x = 10")
       end # if
5 < 10
```

```
julia> x=10
julia> if(x > 10)
           println("$x > 10")
       elseif(x < 10)
           println("$x < 10")
       else                    # because 10 is not > nor < 10
           println("$x = 10")  # this statement gets executed
       end # if
10 = 10
```

The "**elseif**" and "**else**" conditions are optional.

If there is a lot of code between "if" and "elseif" or between "elseif" and "else" or between "else" and "end" that code can be very difficult to read and follow. This might be a case where using an "@goto label" might be useful. For example:

```
julia> function use_goto(x)
       if (x>10)
           @goto greater
       else
           @goto less
       end # if

       @label greater
           println("Greater")    # a long block of code
           @goto jumpout         # skip over the "less" block

       @label less
           println("Less")

       @label jumpout            # all conditions end here
       end # use_goto

julia> use_goto(20)
Greater
julia> use_goto(5)
Less
```

In this example, the **if-else-end** block is like a table of contents. It states where to go if the condition is true. The "@**greater**" and "@**less**" blocks can be very long with no ambiguity as to which conditional block you are in. An additional "@**jumpout**" label is needed so that each conditional block of code ends up in the same place after execution.

if-elseif-else-end blocks are functions and as with other functions they return a value:

```
julia> x = 20
julia> result = if(x>10)
                "greater than"
            else
                "less than"
            end # if

"greater than"

julia> result
"greater than"
```

If the test is an **if-else** conditional, i.e. only two possible outcomes, then the expression can be written using the **ifelse** function.

```
julia> x = 5
julia> result = ifelse(x>10, 2x, 5x)
25
```

If the conditional is true, **ifelse** returns the result of the 2nd expression. If the conditional is false, **ifelse** returns the result of the 3rd expression:

ifelse(test, if true, if false)

Which can be written even more cryptically as in C:

test ? if true : if false

```
julia> x>10 ? 2x : 5x
25
```

If the objective is to execute a statement only if a conditional test is true, then you can use the "and" **&&** syntax. If the conditional test is true, then the expression following the **&&** is evaluated:

```
julia> x=20
julia> x>10 && println("x is > 10")
x is > 10
```

Julia evaluates the first expression, x>10. If that expression is true, then Juia evaluates the second expression, println("x is > 10") and that is what gets returned.

If the conditional test is false, then the expression following the **&&** is not evaluated. Instead the statement returns "false".

```
julia> x = 5
julia> x>10 && println("x is > 10")
false
```

You can also test to see if a conditional is false by using the "or" || syntax:

```
julia> x = 5
julia> x>10 || println("x is not > 10")
x is not > 10
```

In this case Juia evaluates the first expresion. If that expression is true, then there is no need to evaluate the second expression. But, if the first expression is false, then the second expression is evaluated to see if it is true and that is what gets returned.

Julia provides a few built-in tests that return Boolean variables that might be useful when forming **if-elseif-else-end** blocks:

isodd(x::Integer) Returns true if x is odd and false otherwise.

iseven(x::Integer) Returns true is x is even and false otherwise.

isreal(x) Tests whether x is numerically equal to a real number

isinteger(x) Test whether x is numerically equal to some integer. Typeof(x) does not have to be Integer. **isinteger**(4.0) -> true

isempty(collection) Test whether a collection is empty (has no elements).

in(item, collection) Test whether the item is equal to an item in the given collection

It should be noted that all of these tests begin with a lower case ' i ' which is difficult to see in the bold text used here.

Chapter 11

Looping and Iteration

There are many cases where it is required to loop through a block of code and then go back and do it again and again with different conditions each loop. Julia provides a number of ways to implement loops.

11.1 - For-Loops

The basic syntax of a for-loop is:

```
julia> for i = 1:5
           println(" i = $i")
       end # for i
i = 1
i = 2
i = 3
i = 4
i = 5
```

In this expression "1:5" is a range object that evaluates to the sequence of integers 1, 2, 3, 4, 5. Range iterators are frequently used in for-loops. Ranges are specified using the syntax: range = start:step:end. Step is optional and defaults to 1 as in the loop above. For example:

```
julia> r = collect(2:3:8)        # a series of numbers starting with 2 and
3-element Array{Int64,1}:        # ending with 8 with a step size of 3
 2
 5
 8
```

Unlike Python, Julia includes the final range element in the list of numbers.

Although it is possible to use ' = ' in the expression "for i = 1:5" as shown above, it is better to use "in" rather than ' = ':

```
julia> for i in 1:5
           println(" i = $i")
       end # for i
```

As we will see later, there are many versions of for-loops where using "in" makes the statement read more clearly.

It should be noted that the loop variable ' i ', in this case, only exists within the for-loop. As soon as the for-loop ends, the variable ' i ' becomes undefined.

109

Sometimes it is necessary to terminate a for-loop before it completes normally. The "**break**" keyword accomplishes this:

```
julia> for i in 1:1000
           println(" i = $i")
           if i > 4
               break        # exit the loop if 1>4
           end # if
       end # for i
i = 1
i = 2
i = 3
i = 4
i = 5
```

break exits the for-loop immediately.

For nested loops, **break** exits the inner loop containing the **break** keyword but allows the outer loop to continue:

```
julia> for i in 1:2
           for j = 10:15
             println(" i = $i  j = $j")
             if j > 11
               break
             end # if j
           end # for j
       end # for i

i = 1  j = 10
i = 1  j = 11
i = 1  j = 12
i = 2  j = 10
i = 2  j = 11
i = 2  j = 12
```

Nested for loops can also be written using this single line syntax:

```
julia> for i in 1:2, j in 10:12
           println(" i = $i  j = $j")
       end # for i, j

i = 1  j = 10
i = 1  j = 11
i = 1  j = 12
i = 2  j = 10
i = 2  j = 11
i = 2  j = 12
```

If the single line syntax is used, then a break command will exit all of the nested loops:

```
julia> for i in 1:2,  j in 10:12
          println(" i = $i  j = $j")
          if j > 11
             break
          end # if j
       end # for i, j
i = 1  j = 10
i = 1  j = 11
i = 1  j = 12
```

When the condition j >11 is reached the first time, both loops are exited. The second iteration with i = 2 is skipped.

The keyword **continue** is similar to break except that it does not terminate execution of the for-loop as break does:

```
julia> for i in 1:5
          if i<3
             continue
          end # if
          println("i = $i")
       end # for
i = 3
i = 4
i = 5
```

The keyword **continue** causes the for-loop to go to the next loop iteration skipping over any statements between the **continue** and the end of the for-loop.

A key distinction between the for-loop and the while-loop that will be discussed next is that the for-loop is always evaluated at least once.

11.2 - While-Loops

While-loops begin with a conditional test. If that test is true, then the body of the while-loop is executed. The conditional expression is then re-evaluated and once again if it is true the rest of the while-loop is executed. This looping goes on as long as the conditional expression remains true. If the condition expression is false when the while-loop is first reached, the body of the loop is never evaluated.

There are a few critical differences between a for-loop and a while-loop.

1. A for-loop is always evaluated at least one time. A while-loop is never evaluated if the conditional test is false when the while-loop is first encountered.

2. The values of the conditional test parameters, " i " in the following examples, must be changed somewhere in the body of the while-loop in such a way as to make the conditional test false. Else the loop will never stop.

3. The parameters for the conditional expression must be set up before arriving at the while-loop. Else the loop will throw an undefined error.

4. The parameters for the conditional test must be declared "global" inside the while-loop. Else the loop will throw an undefined error.

```
julia> i = 10                    # i defined at the global level

julia> while i <= 12
          println("i = $i")
          global i = i + 1       # i must be defined as global inside the loop
       end # while
i = 10
i = 11
i = 12

julia> i                         # global i has been changed
12
```

The primary reason for ever using a while-loop is if it is required that the loop not be evaluated once.

11.3 - Iteration

Iteration is the process of accessing each element of a collection in order. Iterable objects include tuples, arrays, ranges, sets, dictionaries, and strings. Julia provides a number of ways to make iteration easier.

Here is a basic for-loop used to iterate the elements of an array:

```
julia> a = [10 11 12 13 14];            # a 5 element array

julia> for i in 1:length(a)
          print(a[i],' ')
       end
10 11 12 13 14
```

Here is an easier way to accomplish the same thing using the **eachindex** function:

```
julia> for i in eachindex(a)
          print(a[i],' ')
       end
10 11 12 13 14
```

And here is an even easier way to do it:

```
julia> for item in a
          print(item,' ')
       end
10 11 12 13 14
```

You would use this last style if all you need is the value of the element and not the index of that element. You would use the previous style if you need the index as well as the value of each element.

Here are some other examples of efficient iterators:

```
julia> colors = ["red", "green", "blue"]   # iterate each element in an array
julia> for color in colors
          print(color, ' ')
       end # for
red green blue
```

```
julia> for letter in "Julia"               # iterate each character in a string
          println(letter)
       end
J
u
l
i
a
```

```
julia> t = (5, "Five", 'V')          # a tuple

julia> for element in t              # iterate each element of a tuple
           println(element)
       end # for
5
Five
V
```

Julia provides several efficient iterators for specific applications:

eachline() - Creates an iterable object that will yield each line from a text file. When called with a filename, the file is opened at the beginning of iteration and closed at the end.

```
julia> for line in eachline("my_file.txt")
           print(line)
       end
```

foreach(f, a...) - evaluates the function f for each element of iterable a. For multiple iterable arguments, f is called elementwise.

```
julia> a = [10 11 12]
julia> b = (" = ten", " = eleven", " = twelve")

julia> foreach(println, a, b)          # execute println for each a,b
10 = ten
11 = eleven
12 = twelve
```

Julia provides the "**zip**" function that combines two or more iterable objects of the same size into an array of tuples where the ith element in each tuple contains the ith elements of the original objects.

```
julia> ID    = [11 12 13 14]           # a 4 element array
julia> name = ["sam" "bob" "joe" "tim"]  # another 4 element array
julia> age   = [25 32 18 26]           # another 4 element array

julia> members = zip(ID, name, age)    # zip combines the arrays

julia> for member in members           # iterate thru members
           println(member)
       end

(11, "sam", 25)                        # each member
(12, "bob", 32)
(13, "joe", 18)
(14, "tim", 26)
```

If the iterable objects have different numbers of elements, then the resulting zip object is only as long as the shortest input object.

If you need the index of each element, you can use the **enumerate** function:

```
julia> for (index, member) in enumerate(members)
          println(index,' ',  member)
       end

1 (11, "sam", 25)
2 (12, "bob", 32)
3 (13, "joe", 18)
4 (14, "tim", 26)
```

If you want to convert an input array into an output array, you can use an array "comprehension".

output_array = [2x^2 for x in input_array]

where 2x^2 is an example. It could be any anonymous function.

11.4 - Iterating 2-dim Arrays

The elements in a 2-dimensional array are not actually stored in computer memory as a 2-dimensional array of numbers. Insofar as possible the array data will be stored in sequential memory addresses. That is, the data are stored in a quasi 1-dimensional array in computer memory. The first data stored will be row1, row2, row3,... for column 1. Then row1, row2, row3,... for column 2 and so forth. Because of this storage architecture it has been posited that it will be faster to access a 2-dim array by iterating down rows first and across columns second:

```
for col = ...
  for row = ...
     ...
  end # row loop
end # col loop
```

This is probably true if the array data is stored on a disk drive because of the time needed to reposition the read-head. However, it may not be true for a solid state drive (SSD). To test this hypothesis I ran the following test on my computer using an SSD.

First, create an array with 2500 elements arranged as a 10 row by 250 column array:

```
julia> a = collect(1:2500);       # create a 1x2500 1-dim array
julia> b = reshape(a, (10,250));   # reshape into a 10x250 2-dim array
```

115

A simple function, addup1(), iterates through the array adding each element to a sum. This version iterates the "wrong" way by cycling through columns first:

```
julia> function addup1(b)
         sum = 0
         for row in 1:10
           for col in 1:250
             sum = sum + b[row,col]
           end # for col
         end # for row
       end # function addup1
```

The @**elapsed** macro measures the time taken to execute the **addup1**() function.

```
julia> @elapsed addup1(b)
0.009926937 sec
```

The time to execute the function the first time: 9.9 msec, includes the time needed to compile the code. The second time the @elapsed macro is run yields the time for the already compiled code to run ~ 3.2 μsec:

```
julia> @elapsed addup1(b)
3.251e-6 sec
```

A second function, addup2(), was written iterating the "right" way by cycling through rows first:

```
julia> function addup2(b)
         sum = 0
         for col in 1:250
           for row in 1:10
             sum = sum + b[row,col]
           end # for row
         end # for col
       end # function addup2
```

The second time the @**elapsed** macro was run on addup2 yielded an execution time of 3.6 μsec.

```
julia> @elapsed addup2(b)
3.61e-6 sec
```

This simple example would seem to indicate that it doesn't make a significant difference in execution time whether you iterate through a 2-dim array the "right" way or the "wrong" way if your data are stored on an SSD. It might make a significant difference if your data are stored on a mechanical disk drive.

Chapter 12

Input/Output

All useful code accepts input data and produces output data. Input data can be read from a data file stored on a disk drive somewhere or it can come from a human operator typing on stdin. Output data can be written to a text or data file or it can be "printed" to stdout. We will discuss all of this in this chapter.

12.1 - Changing the Working Directory

Before you create a file or try to read from a file, you need to be sure that you are in the proper directory. By default the REPL works at the top level of the current user. You can change the working directory using the REPL shell mode. To enter the shell mode, type a semicolon at the Julia prompt. You have to do this for each shell command.

Type a semicolon to enter shell mode

| julia> ;

The cd command changes the working directory. On macOS the tilde character, ~, represents the top level of the current user, /Users/GRRoot/ in my case.

| shell> cd ~/Documents/Julia/"Julia Code"

The new working directory is:

| /Users/GRRoot/Documents/Julia/Julia Code

Type a semicolon to enter shell mode

| julia> ;

The ls command lists the contents of the working directory

```
shell> ls          # list the contents of the current working directory
myFile.txt         # myfile.txt is the only file in this directory
```

From here on REPL statements will be executed in this directory.

The table on the next page shows a few of the shell commands available on macOS and other UNIX based machines. Of these, the pwd (print working directory) and cd (change working directory) commands will be most useful for directing your input and output commands to the proper location in your file system.

If you are using the Jupyter Notebook environment, your working directory will be the one containing your Notebook (.ipynb) file.

Enter Shell Mode by Typing a Semicolon at the Julia Prompt		
Common Shell Commands		
cd	change directory	Changes the current working directory to the specified path.
ls	List	Displays the contents of the specified directory (or the current directory if no path is specified).
mkdir	Make Directory	Creates a new directory.
pwd	Print Working Directory	Displays the full path of the current directory.
rm	Remove	Deletes the specified file or files.
Ctrl-C	Abort	Sends an abort signal to the current command.

12.2 - Writing to a Binary Data File

As an example we first create a 3x3 array of Int64 numbers. These numbers actually represent the indices (row,col) of their locations in the array. Since we intend to write this array to a binary file, we name the array "array_out".

```
julia> array_out = [11 12 13 ; 21 22 23 ; 31 32 33]
3×3 Array{Int64,2}:
 11  12  13
 21  22  23
 31  32  33
```

Now we open() an IOStream named io_out linked to an external file named "mydata. dat" for writing. If that file does not exist, the open() function will create it.

```
julia> io_out = open("mydata.dat", "w")
IOStream(<file mydata.dat>)
```

A simple write() function writes the entire array_out to the IOStream. In this case the write() function returns 72 equal to the number of bytes written.

```
julia> write(io_out, array_out)          # write(to, from)
72
```

Closing the IOStream "io_out" flushes the IO buffer to the external file and then breaks the link between that IOStream and the external file.

```
julia> close(io_out)
```

12.3 - Reading from a Binary Data File

Since the external file contains binary data, it is impossible for Julia to know what data Type those binary data represent. We have to give Julia a "template" for the file data contents. In this case, the file contains a 3x3 array of Int64 numbers that we have named array_out. We need to create a template for an array "similar" to this array. The similar() function does this.

The following statement creates a new array in memory, "array_in", that has the same dimensions and the same data Type as the argument array, "array_out" in this case. The similar() function does not copy the actual data. In fact it does not fill the new array with anything. As a result, the new array contains whatever garbage was left over from the previous use of those memory locations.

> julia> array_in = **similar**(array_out)
> 3×3 Array{Int64,2}:

Now we can open() the external file containing the binary data for reading and attach it to the IOStream io_in:

> julia> io_in = **open**("mydata.dat","r")
> IOStream(<file mydata.dat>)

A simple **read!**() statement (note the exclamation point !) transfers the file data to the template aray:

> julia> **read!**(io_in, array_in)
> 3×3 Array{Int64,2}:
> 11 12 13
> 21 22 23
> 31 32 33

And finally we close() the IOStream:

> julia> **close**(io_in)   # this happens automatically when EOF is reached

To demonstrate that the stored binary data do not contain any indication of what those data represent, we can form a fictitious 1-dim array with 9 elements:

> julia> **array_new** = [1 2 3 4 5 6 7 8 9]
> 1 2 3 4 5 6 7 8 9

Now open an IOStream pointing to the "mydata.dat" file that was written to contain a 3x3 2-dim array of integers.

> julia> io_in = open("mydata.dat","r")

Read the file into the 1-dim array:

> julia> read!(io_in, **array_new**)
> 11 21 31 12 22 32 13 23 33

The same data can be read and displayed as 1-dim, 2-dim, or n-dim. These constructs are only useful as an aid for the user in visualizing the data. The representation in computer memory is the same.

12.4 - Printing Output

Probably the most common output operation is printing text to stdout so that the user can see the results of computations. Unfortunately, Julia printing is a work in progress so there are a few speed bumps to master.

The basic Julia printing functions are **print**() and its companion **println**(). The only difference is that the **println**() function adds a newline character (\n) to the end of each String printed.

> julia> **print**("This is a String")
> This is a String
> julia> **println**("This is a String")
> This is a String
>   # println() has added a newline after the String

You can insert a numerical value into the printed string using the dollar sign (**$**) placeholder:

> julia> **println**("pi = $pi")
> pi = π = 3.1415926535897...

You can insert the values of variables and simple math operations directly in the println() command:

> julia> a = 2
> julia> b = 4
> julia> **println**("$a x $b = $(a*b)")
> 2 x 4 = 8

The dollar sign placeholder automatically formats the numbers it prints in a "pleasant" way but does not provide any way to change that formatting. Julia provides a macro, @printf() that does allow formatting using C style format specifiers. But, @printf() has a number of limitations that limit its usefulness. The first is that it is not provided as part of the standard Julia installation. You have to add the **Printf** package using the Julia pkg manager.

> julia> **]**   # type a left bracket to launch the pkg manager
> (v1.0) pkg> **add** Printf   # add the Printf package
> (v1.0) pkg> **delete**   # press the delete key to return to Julia
> julia> **using** Printf   # type "using Printf" to complete the installation

You can now print formatted numerical values in Strings using the @printf() macro. @printf format specifiers start with '%'.

> julia> **@printf**("π = %8.3f",pi)
> π =   3.142
> julia> **@printf** "π = %8.3f" pi
> π =   3.142

These two statements do the same thing, but they are not the same. The @printf() macro has two syntaxes as illustrated above. You can use parentheses around the arguments with commas inside the parentheses, or leave out both parentheses and commas.

The syntax without parentheses and commas allows printing more than a single number but is incredibly difficult to read:

> julia> @printf "π = %6.3f 2*pi = %6.3f" pi 2*pi
> π = 3.142 2*pi = 6.283

The syntax using parentheses and commas, while easier to read, doesn't work for more than a single number.

> julia> @printf ("π = %6.3f 2*pi = %6.3f", pi, 2*pi)
> ERROR: LoadError: ArgumentError:

The String "%6.3f" in these printf() statements is a format specifier. Julia uses the same format specifiers as does the C language and many others. The most useful of these format specifiers are summarized in the table below. Examples follow.

%[flags][width][.precision][number type]

[flags]	Meaning
-	left justified in field
+	forces + before positive numbers
space	forces blank space where a + would appear
0	left pad the field with zeros

[width]	Meaning
integer	total width (all characters) in field width includes sign, decimal point exponent 'e' or 'E'

[precision]	Meaning
integer	number of digits following the decimal point

[number type]	Meaning
d or i	signed decimal integer
u	unsigned decimal integer
f or F	floating point decimal number
e or E	exponential notation decimal number
g	use the shorter of e or f
G	use the shorter of E or F
c	a single Character
s	String

> julia> @printf "The value of pi = %10.5f \n" pi
> The value of pi =   **3.14159**

julia> @printf "The value of pi = **%-10.5f \ n**" pi
The value of pi = **3.14159**

julia> @printf "The value of pi = **%+10.5f \n**" pi
The value of pi =   **+3.14159**

julia> @printf "The value of pi = **%010.5f \n**" pi
The value of pi = **0003.14159**

julia> @printf "The value of pi = **%-10.3F \n**" pi
The value of pi = **3.142**

julia> @printf "The value of pi = **%-10.3e \n**" pi
The value of pi = **3.142e+00**

julia> @printf "The value of pi = **%-10.3E \n**" pi
The value of pi = **3.142E+00**

julia> @printf "The value of pi = **%-10.3G \n**" pi
The value of pi = **3.14**

julia> @printf "The value of pi = **%-10.3g \n**" pi
The value of pi = **3.14**

The 'g" and 'G' specifiers don't work properly. Fortunately they are not needed.

So, we have seen that the macro version @printf() doesn't always work, but there is an even more fatal flaw: the format specifier must appear as a literal String in the macro argument list. You cannot define a format specifier as a String and then use that String in the @printf() statement.

julia> **fmt** = "The value of pi = %10.5f\n"

julia> @printf(**fmt**,pi)
ERROR: LoadError: ArgumentError: @printf: first or second argument must be a format string

julia> typeof(fmt)
String

The variable "fmt" is a String, but it doesn't work in the @printf() macro which apparently doesn't recognize it as a String.

Fortunately, Julia provides a package that implements formatting using format specifier strings and that will be described next.

The "Format" Package

The Julia **Format** package provides both C style and Python style number formatting. To add this package, follow these steps which should be getting familiar by now:

julia>]	# type a left bracket to launch the pkg manager
(v1.0) pkg> **add** Format	# add the Format package
(v1.0) pkg> **delete**	# press the delete key to return to Julia
julia> **using** Format	# type "using Format"

C Style Formatting

The **Format** package allows **C** style format strings to be used although in a somewhat cumbersome way:

Start by defining a format string using the **C** format syntax:

julia> fmt_str = "%-10.3f"

The **cfmt**() function uses the C format string to format a number. The result is a String containing the number converted according to the format specification.

julia> str_pi = **cfmt**(fmt_str,pi)   # convert π to a String using fmt_str
"3.142   "

Now the Julia standard println() function can be used to print ancillary text and the String version of the number.

julia> **println**("The value of π = ", str_pi)
The value of π = 3.142

It is not necessary to convert the number into a String separately.

julia> println("The value of π = ", cfmt(fmt_str,pi))
The value of π = 3.142

However, it is not possible to include the format string directly in the cfmt() argument list:

julia> println("The value of π = ", cfmt("%-10.3",pi))
ERROR: ArgumentError: invalid printf format string: "%-10.3"

Using the cfmt() function it would be possible to convert several numbers into Strings and then to concatenate those Strings in a single String to be printed but this seems to be unnecessarily cumbersome.

Using Python style formatting is more fully developed in Julia v1.0 and that will be discussed next.

Python Style Formatting

The **Format** package also allows **Python** style format strings to be used. This might be the easier way if you are coming from a Python background.

Python format specifiers work somewhat like the standard Julia $ syntax. In standard Julia $ formatting, the $ symbol precedes the name of a variable. When a println() function prints a String with an $name item in that String, the $name item is replaced with a string representation of the numerical variable named "name" as in the following example.

> julia> **var_a** = 45.678   # define a variable named 'var_a'

In the following println() function call, the String "**$var_a**" is replaced with the numerical value of var_a.

> julia> println("var_a = **$var_a**")
> **var_a** = 45.678

Python style formatting works in a similar fashion as illustrated in the following example:

Define a Python style format expression:

> julia> fmt_exp = **FormatExpr**("var_a = {:<8.4f}");

In fmt_exp the sub-string "{:<8.4}" represents a format specifier that will be applied to the first variable in the argument list for a subsequent **printfmt()** function call:

> julia> **printfmt**(fmt_exp, **var_a**);
> var_a = 45.6780

Note that each of the preceding two function calls have been appended with a semicolon (;) to suppress additional output generated by the functions.

Multiple variables can be printed with a single printfmt() call by defining a suitable FormatExpr().

> julia> fmt_abc = FormatExpr("a = {:<3d} b = {:<6.2f} c = {:<6.2f}");
> julia> printfmt(fmt_abc, a, b, c);
> a = 10 b = 20.50 c = 39.80

This ability to separate the format string from the printfmt() function is critical for producing readable code. The FormatExp() statement can be very long and involved while the printfmt() function call can be shorter and more readable.

We have been using format specifiers such as {:<3d} and {:<6.2f} without explaining what they mean. These Python format specifiers are actually very similar to the C style formatting specifiers you may be more familiar with - they just use different symbols to accomplish the same purpose.

The syntax for Julia Python style formatting specifiers is described in the table on the next page.

{[:[fill]align]][sign][width][,][.precision][type]}

[[fill]align]	Meaning
<	left justified in field
>	right justified in field
fill	any character to fill empty spaces. space = default
0	left pad the field with zeros

sign	Meaning
+	show + for positive numbers
-	show sign (-) for negative numbers only
space	insert space instead of + for positive numbers

[width]	Meaning
integer	total width (all characters) in field width includes sign, decimal point exponent 'e' or 'E'

[,]	Meaning
,	use commas to separate thousands

[precision]	Meaning
integer	number of digits following the decimal point

[number type]	Meaning
d or i	signed decimal integer
f or F	floating point decimal number
e or E	exponential notation decimal number

All Python style format specifiers are enclosed in curly braces { }. These format specifiers can be numbered if there is more than one in a single Format Expression

```
julia> fmt_abc = FormatExpr("a = {1:<3d} b = {2:<6.2f} c = {3:<6.2f} \n");
```

The numbers are optional. **The colons are required**. If no numbers are given, the first specifier will be applied to the first variable in the argument list and so forth.

There are several examples of formatting using **FormatExpr** on the next page. The character 'I' has been inserted before and after the formatted field so that you can see where the field starts an ends.

```
julia> b = 2.5;          # define a real number
julia> s = "string";     # define a string

julia> fmt = FormatExpr("b = |{1:<8.2f}| \n"); printfmt(fmt,b);
b = |2.50    |          # left aligned in 8 character field

julia> fmt = FormatExpr("b = |{1:0>8.2f}| \n"); printfmt(fmt,b);
b = |00002.50|          # right aligned filled with 0's

julia> fmt = FormatExpr("b = |{1:·>8.2f}| \n"); printfmt(fmt,b);
b = |····2.50|          # right aligned filled with ·

julia> fmt = FormatExpr("b = |{1:·<8.2f}| \n"); printfmt(fmt,b);
b = |2.50····|          # left aligned filled with ·

julia> fmt = FormatExpr("b = |{1:·<8.2e}| \n"); printfmt(fmt,b);
b = |2.50e+00|          # left aligned exponential notation

julia> fmt = FormatExpr("s = |{1:·>10s}| \n"); printfmt(fmt,s);
b = |····string|        # right aligned string filled with ·

julia> m = 1000000;     # define a large number

julia> fmt = FormatExpr("m = |{1:>12.2e}| \n"); printfmt(fmt,m);
m = |    1.00e+06|      # right aligned exponential 'e' notation

julia> fmt = FormatExpr("m = |{1:>12.2E}| \n"); printfmt(fmt,m);
m = |    1.00E+06|      # right aligned exponential 'E' notation

julia> fmt = FormatExpr("m = |{1:>6.2f}| \n"); printfmt(fmt,m);
m = |1000000.00|        # field 6.2 expands to 10.2

julia> fmt = FormatExpr("m = |{1:>.2f}| \n"); printfmt(fmt,m);
m = |1000000.00|        # unspecified field expands as needed
```

Note that the field width specified is actually the minimum width. Fields will expand automatically if needed to represent the number. So, if what you want is for the number to just fill the field, you can simply use a field width = 1 and let Julia take care of figuring out what the real field width should be:

```
julia> fmt = FormatExpr("π = {1:1.4f}");          # specified width = 1
julia> printfmt(fmt,π);

π = 3.1416              # actual field width = 6 characters

julia> fmt = FormatExpr("π = {1:1.4e}");          # specified width = 1
julia> printfmt(fmt,π);

π = 3.1416e+00          # actual field width = 10 characters
```

12.5 - Writing to a Text File

Before you can write to or read from a text file, you have to "open" that file. One syntax for the open function is:

open(filename, [mode]) -> IOStream

where filename is a text string giving the name of a text file. The mode specifier is optional and defaults to "r" if not specified. Mode specifiers are listed below with their full meanings:

- "r"   read - read from an existing file
- "w"   write, create, truncate
- "a"   write, create, append
- "r+"   read, write
- "w+"   read, write, create, truncate
- "a+"   read, write, create, append

Note that the mode specifiers are strings even if they contain only a single character.

- The keywords with "create" will create the specified file if it does not already exist.
- The "truncate" keyword truncates (erases) the file to zero size
- The "append" keyword moves the insertion point to the end of the existing file so that a subsequent write will write to the end of the file.

The open() function attaches an external file to an IOStream buffer in memory. When you write to that file, what you write gets accumulated in the IOBuffer in memory. Those buffer contents are actually written to the external file from time to time. When you are done writing, it is important that you close the IOStream. This will flush the internal buffer to the external file and ensure that all of what you wrote actually gets to the file. Every "open()" should be followed by a "close()" when file operations are finished.

Here's an example of simple code that writes Strings to a text file:

    julia> outfile = open("myfile.txt", "w")

This statement creates the file "myfile.txt" if it does not exist. The open() function returns an IOStream identifier. In this case that IOStream is named "outfile". You can now write to the IOStream. If the second argument of the write() function is a String, that String will be written to the text file.

    julia> write(outfile,"This is the first line of text \n")
    julia> write(outfile,"This is the second line of text \n")
    julia> close(outfile)   # closes the IOStream "outfile" and the file "myfile.txt"

At this point the file myfile.txt contains two lines of text:

This is the first line of text
This is the second line of text

12.6 - Reading from a Text File

Continuing from the previous example:

| julia> infile = open("myFile.txt", "r")

This open() function opens an existing file in read mode and attaches that file to an IOStream buffer named "infile".

| julia> read(infile, String)

This version of the read() function reads and returns the entire file contents into a single Type String variable.

    "This is the first line of text \nThis is the second line of text \n"
    julia> close(infile)

Well, that worked but it concatenated all of the file contents into a single String. Probably not what you wanted. Julia provides an efficient iterator for stepping through a text file line-by-line:

```
julia> infile = open("myfile.txt", "r")
julia> for line in eachline(infile)
        println(line)
      end

This is the first line of text
This is the second line of text

julia> close(infile)
```

The **"for line in eachline(file)"** construct is very useful. It combines iteration and parsing the input data into individual lines of text all in one short statement.

You can use the **"append"** mode to add to the end of an existing file:

```
julia> outfile = open("myfile.txt", "a")
julia> write(outfile,"This is the third line of text \n")
julia> write(outfile,"This is the forth line of text \n")
julia> close(outfile)
```

The file "myfile.txt" now contains 4 lines of text:

```
julia> infile = open("myfile.txt", "r")
julia> for line in eachline(infile)
        println(line)
      end

This is the first line of text
This is the second line of text
This is the third line of text
This is the forth line of text

julia> close(infile)
```

12.7 - Reading and Writing Delimited Files

Julia provides functions for writing and reading delimited text files. A "delimited file" is a text file wherein each line of text contains 2 or more data items separated by a "delimiter". The two most common delimiters are commas and tab characters ('\t'). A special text file extension, ".csv", is used to identify files containing comma separated values. Tab delimited files usually have file extension ".txt" indicating a simple text file. Tab delimited files are preferred if the file data are to be printed because the columns of data line up nicely and are easier to read.

There are two common types of delimited text files:

1. Data arrays = arrays of data without a header row. Simple data arrays were described in Chapter 7. In this chapter we will discuss reading and writing data arrays from/to delimited text files.

2. DataFrames = arrays of data with a header row giving column names. DataFrames were described in detail in Chapter 8. In this chapter we will discuss reading and writing DataFrames from/to delimited text files.

Julia provides several packages that facilitate reading and writing delimited text files. There is some duplication of functionality between these packages. In this chapter we will discuss only two of these packages:

1. **CSV** - This is the package to use for reading and writing DataFrames.

2. **DelimitedFiles** - This is the package to use for reading and writing simple data arrays without header rows.

There is some redundancy between these packages. The primary distinguisher is their suitability for use with data arrays and with DataFrames. As indicated, the CSV package is most suited for reading and writing DataFrames.

12.7.1 - Reading DataFrame Files Using CSV:

The Julia package CSV is designed primarily for reading and writing DataFrames. It can read a simple data array with no header row, but it creates a header row and converts the array into a DataFrame. This is not good.

In order to read and write DataFrames it is necessary to add the **CSV** pkg:

```
julia> ]
(v1.0) pkg> add CSV
julia> Delete
julia> using CSV
```

The syntax for the CSV read function is:

CSV.read(path,sink=DataFrame; kwargs...)

where:

- **path** = path to the text file to be read

- **sink** = any valid Tables.jl sink. Defaults to **DataFrame** and that is the only option to be discussed here. For this reason, the sink parameter will be left out of the function calls.

Some useful key word arguments are:

- **header** = row or range of rows to use as the header for the DataFrame.The header row typically contains the names of the DataFrame columns. Defaults to 1 and this is the only value that will be used in the following examples.
- **datarow** = the row where the data starts. Defaults to the row after the header row.
- **skipto** = the number of rows to skip before starting to read data
- **footerskip** = the number of rows to skip at the end of the file
- **delim** = the character to use as the delimiter between data elements. Defaults to delim=',' indicating a coma delimited file. Can also be '\t' indication a tab delimited file

There are others and you might want to read the documentation on CSV if you need some additional functionality.

Because the default values are all applicable for the examples to be shown, the CSV.read syntax can be simplified for our purposes:

CSV.read("fileName"; **delim**=',')

I have retained the delim=',' kwarg even though it is not necessary for working with comma delimited files. However, it is necessary to work with tab delimited files which I will also discuss.

Reading Comma Delimited DataFrames:

DF_Comma.csv is a comma delimited text file containing an array of Int64 with one header row containing column names:

```
☼  ~/Documents/Julia/Julia Code/DF_Comma.csv ▾
1   Name1,Name2,Name3,Name4
2   11,21,31,41
3   12,22,32,42
4   13,23,33,43
```

The header row contains comma separated names, "Name1", "Name2", ..., for each column of data. This file can be read with a simple call to **CSV.read**:

```
julia> df = CSV.read("DF_Comma.csv")
3×4 DataFrame
```

| Row | Name1 | Name2 | Name3 | Name4 |
	Int64	Int64	Int64	Int64
1	11	21	31	41
2	12	22	32	42
3	13	23	33	43

Reading Tab Delimited DataFrames:

DF_Tab.txt is a tab ('\t') delimited text file containing an array of Int64 with one header row containing column names. In this figure, tabs are indicated by the small triangles separating the data items.

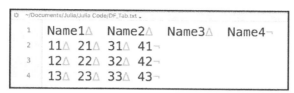

```
julia> df = CSV.read("DF_Tab.txt"; delim='\t')
3x4 DataFrame
```

| Row | Name1 | Name2 | Name3 | Name4 |
	Int64⍰	Int64⍰	Int64⍰	Int64⍰
1	11	21	31	41
2	12	22	32	42
3	13	23	33	43

The CSV.read function correctly reads DataFrame text files delimited by commas and by tabs. In addition, it can read tab delimited text files with .txt file name extension.

The CSV.read function can also read text data files without header rows, but it converts the first row of data into a header row and then converts the result into a DataFrame.

```
julia> df = CSV.read("DF_NoHeader.csv")
2x4 DataFrame
```

| Row | 11 | 21 | 31 | 41 |
	Int64⍰	Int64⍰	Int64⍰	Int64⍰
1	12	22	32	42
2	13	23	33	43

In order to properly read delimited text files that contain simple data arrays with no header rows, a different Julia function is needed. This function is included in the **DelimitedFiles** package.

12.7.2 - Reading Data Files Using DelimitedFiles:

The **DelimitedFiles** package contains functions for reading and writing delimited text files using commas and tabs as delimiter characters. These files should contain data arrays without header rows.

Add the **DelimitedFiles** pkg:

> julia>]
> (v1.0) pkg> add **DelimitedFiles**
> julia> Delete
> julia> using **DelimitedFiles**

The DelimitedFiles package contains a function, **readdlm()** that can be used to read delimited text files delimited by commas or tabs. The syntax is:

readdlm(path,delimiter, Type, end-of-line character)

where:

- **path** = path to the text file to be read
- **delimiter** = the character used to delimit the data items. If the delimiter is not given, it defaults to white space including tab.
- **Type** = data type in the array. If the data type is not given it defaults to Float64 for numbers. A Type of ANY can be used for heterogeneous data arrays.
- **end-of-line character** = If the eol character is not given it defaults to '\n'.

Thus, it is very simple to read tab delimited data files that satisfy these defaults:

readdlm(path)

Reading Comma Delimited Data Files:

Data.csv is a comma delimited text file containing an array of Int64:

```
☼  ~/Documents/Julia/Julia Code/Data.csv ▾
1   11,21,31,41
2   12,22,32,42
3   13,23,33,43
```

This file can be read using the readdlm() function. It is necessary to specify the delimiter character as a comma ',' because the default is white space. Because the data type was not specified, numerical data are converted to Float64.

> julia> data = **readdlm**("Data.csv", ',')
> 3×4 Array{Float64,2}:
>
> 11.0 21.0 31.0 41.0
> 12.0 22.0 32.0 42.0
> 13.0 23.0 33.0 43.0

Reading Tab Delimited Data Files:

Data.txt is a tab ('\t') delimited text file containing an array of Int64. In this figure, tabs are indicated by the small triangles separating the data items.

```
⚙  ~/Documents/Julia/Julia Code/Data.txt ₋
1    11△ 21△ 31△ 41¬
2    12△ 22△ 32△ 42¬
3    13△ 23△ 33△ 43¬
```

If the delimiter is not given in a call to readdlm(), it defaults to white space including the tab character. If the data type is not given it defaults to Float64 for numbers. If the eol character is not given it defaults to '\n'. Thus, it is very simple to read delimited files that satisfy these defaults:

```
julia> data = readdlm("Data.txt")
3×4 Array{Float64,2}:

 11.0  21.0  31.0  41.0
 12.0  22.0  32.0  42.0
 13.0  23.0  33.0  43.0
```

Reading DataFrame Files Using DelimitedFiles:

The **readdlm**() function can read text files with header rows but it is necessary to add a keyword argument to the function call. The **header=true** keyword argument tells **readdlm**() that the text file contains a header row.

```
julia> data = readdlm("DF_Tab.txt"; header=true)        # note the ;

([11.0 21.0 31.0 41.0; 12.0 22.0 32.0 42.0; 13.0 23.0 33.0 43.0],
AbstractString["Name1" "Name2" "Name3" "Name4"])
```

When the readdlm() function reads a file containing a header, it returns the data as a simple array and the header row as a separate tuple of column names. The data array can be recovered as:

```
julia> array = data[1]
3×4 Array{Float64,2}:

 11.0  21.0  31.0  41.0
 12.0  22.0  32.0  42.0
 13.0  23.0  33.0  43.0
```

Individual elements of the data array can be recovered as usual:

```
julia> row = 2
julia> col  = 3
julia> array[row,col]
32.0
```

12.7.3 - Writing DataFrame Files Using CSV:

The **CSV** package contains the **CSV.write**() function for writing DataFrame text files using commas or tabs as delimiter characters. The syntax is quite simple:

CSV.write(path,file; kwargs...)

The only key word argument of interest here is **delim**= a character or String to use to delimit data items in the output file. This is only needed to write tab delimited files since comma delimiters is the default.

The DataFrame df is left over from a previous example and can be reused here:

```
julia> df
3×4 DataFrame

| Row | Name1  | Name2  | Name3  | Name4  |
|     | Int64□ | Int64□ | Int64□ | Int64□ |
├─────┼────────┼────────┼────────┼────────┤
| 1   | 11     | 21     | 31     | 41     |
| 2   | 12     | 22     | 32     | 42     |
| 3   | 13     | 23     | 33     | 43     |
```

This DataFrame can be written to a delimited text file using CSV.write():

```
julia> CSV.write("outfile.csv", df)        # text file, source
"outfile.csv"
```

This writes the DataFrame to the text file "outfile.csv" where it can be opened using a text editor:

```
☼  ~/Documents/Julia/Julia Code/outfile.csv ▾
1   Name1,Name2,Name3,Name4
2   11,21,31,41
3   12,22,32,42
4   13,23,33,43
```

Since no delimiter character was specified, the default comma was used. It is also possible to write a tab delimited file by specifying the '\t' delimiter.

```
julia> CSV.write("outfile.txt", df; delim='\t')
"outfile.txt"
```

```
☼  ~/Documents/Julia/Julia Code/outfile.txt ▾
1   Name1△  Name2△  Name3△  Name4¬
2   11△ 21△ 31△ 41¬
3   12△ 22△ 32△ 42¬
4   13△ 23△ 33△ 43¬
```

12.7.4 - Writing Data Files Using DelimitedFiles:

Writing data files that do not contain header rows requires use of a different write function. Just as the DelimitedFiles readdlm() function was best suited for reading this type of file, so the DelimitedFiles **writedlm**() function is best for writing this type of file.

Using the default tab '\t' delimiter results in a simple writedlm() function call:

| julia> **writedlm**("dlm.txt", array)

This is the resulting text file:

```
☼  ~/Documents/Julia/Julia Code/dlm.txt ↴
 1    11.0△    21.0△    31.0△    41.0¬
 2    12.0△    22.0△    32.0△    42.0¬
 3    13.0△    23.0△    33.0△    43.0¬
```

Writing a comma delimited file:

| julia> **writedlm**("dlm.csv", array, ',')   # note the comma delimiter

This writedlm() function results in the creation of this comma delimited text file:

```
☼  ~/Documents/Julia/Julia Code/dlm.csv ↴
 1   |11.0,21.0,31.0,41.0
 2    12.0,22.0,32.0,42.0
 3    13.0,23.0,33.0,43.0
```

Chapter 13

Making Line & Scatter Plots

Julia provides a number of plotting packages to choose from. One of the best is **PyPlot** which provides a link to the Python plotting package **Matplotlib**. Because of this heritage, Julia plotting using PyPlot is very well documented and is easy to learn. PyPlot runs both in REPL interactive mode and in the Jupyter Notebook environment. The PyPlot package allows you to call Python Matplotlib functions using a slightly modified syntax that I will describe.

In this chapter I will provide an introduction to PyPlot that will be sufficient for many plotting tasks. For more information about Matplotlib, the book "**Matplotlib for Python Developers 2nd Edition**" by Aldrin Yin, et al, and published by PACKT Publishing is available from Amazon. I should mention that many of the PACKT Publishing books on Julia are out of data and do not provide useful information commensurate to their price. For a less expensive reference here is the "official" website:

https://github.com/JuliaPy/PyPlot.jl

There are many other websites that offer information on plotting in Julia, but many of these sites are out of date and the code examples they provide don't work.

13.1 - Installing "PyPlot" in the Julia REPL

PyPlot plotting functions are not included as part of the Base Julia installation and must be added using the Julia package manager (pkg). Start by typing a right-square-bracket ( ]) at the julia prompt:

```
julia> ]                    # this launches the pkg manager
(v1.0) pkg> add PyPlot      # add "PyPlot"
delete                      # press the delete key
julia> using PyPlot         # returns you to the Julia prompt
```

When you use the pkg manager to add PyPlot, or any package for that matter, Julia goes out to the github repository and downloads the PyPlot package. It then compiles that package, so this whole process may take several minutes depending upon Internet traffic. Be patient. If the Julia prompt has not appeared, the job is not finished.

We will also need the DataFrames package described in Chapter 8 for these examples.

```
(v1.0) pkg> add DataFrames
julia> using DataFrames
```

137

13.2 - Generating Data to Plot

Before we plot some data, we have to have some data to plot. **PyPlot** assumes data in array format. Some other plotting packages, Gadfly in particular, want data in DataFrame format. I will show how to generate both types of data using previously described Julia functions.

We will start by creating an array of data representing angles from 0 to 90 degrees:

```
|    julia> Angle = collect(0.0:2.0:90.0);    # array of angles in degrees
```

Compute an array containing the sine of those angles:

```
|    julia> Sine = [sind(angle) for angle in Angle];
```

The **sind()** function takes angles in degrees. These statements were ended with a semicolon to suppress printing of function output.

Similarly:

```
|    julia> Cosine = [cosd(angle) for angle in Angle];
```

At this point we have three arrays representing angles and the sine and cosine of those angles. We can combine these arrays into a DataFrame. Start by creating an empty DataFrame:

```
|    julia> df = DataFrame();
```

We can now add a column to the empty DataFrame:

```
|    julia> df[:Angle] = Angle;
```

This statement defines a new column in df with the name **:Angle**. The colon before Angle indicates that this text is a Symbol to be used as the name of the first column in the DataFrame df. The second and third columns are similarly added:

```
julia> df[:Sine] = Sine;
julia> df[:Cosine] = Cosine;
```

We now have three separate arrays of data and one DataFrame that contains all of these data.

```
julia> df
```

| Row | Angle | Sine | Cosine |
	Float64	Float64	Float64
1	0.0	0.0	1.0
2	2.0	0.0348995	0.999391
3	4.0	0.0697565	0.997564
4	6.0	0.104528	0.994522
5	8.0	0.139173	0.990268

If your data source is a DataFrame and you want to use PyPlot to plot those data, you can extract each column of data:

julia> angle_array = **df[:Angle]**

0.0
2.0
4.0
...

We now have some data to plot.

13.3 - Generating a Simple Plot

The syntax for creating a simple line plot in the REPL is:

| julia> **plot**(Angle, Sine)

Here is the resulting plot of array Sine vs the array Angle:

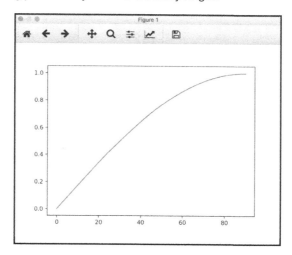

This plot is fully interactive. You can make adjustments to the default plot using the menu items listed across the top of the plot and illustrated below:

Figure 13-1

- The icon labeled "**1**" in **Figure 13-1** allows you to save the plot in a variety of image formats:

    The default is *.png but you can choose other formats including *.pdf and *.svg as shown on the next page. Give the file a name and click on "Save".

139

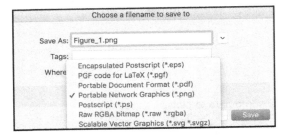

- The icon at **"2"** in **Figure 13-1** allows you to choose options for the plot axes and the plotted curve itself. The axes options are shown at the left and the curve options are shown at the right in this figure:

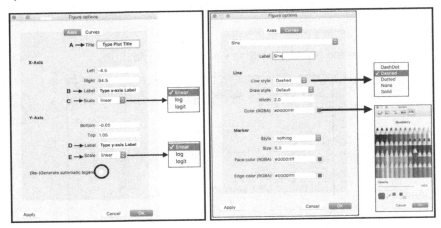

In the **Axes** options panel shown at the left:

- You can enter a title for the plot at "A"
- You can enter text to be used as the x and y axes labels at "B" and "D"
- You can choose log, linear, or logit axes for the x and y axes at "C"and "E"
- If you click the check-box shown circled, a legend will be added to the plot containing the labels you have assigned to each curve in the plot.

In the **Curves** options panel shown at the right above:

- You can choose which curve you want to edit using the drop-down menu
- You can change the label for the chosen curve
- You can choose the line style
- You can choose a color for the curve

- The icon at **"3"** in **Figure 13-1** allows you to choose options for the size of the plot and how the plot fits in the plot panel. You can also change the size and aspect ratio of the plot by clicking on the lower-right corner of the plot window and dragging as illustrated on the next page.

The size and aspect ratio of the plot frame have been changed by dragging the lower-right corner of the plot.

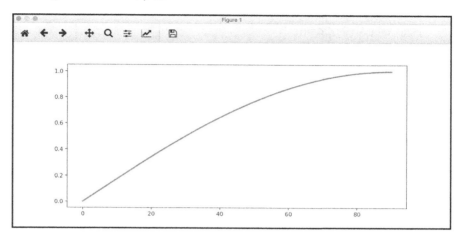

- The magnifying glass and cross arrows icons shown in **Figure 13-1** allow you to zoom in on a portion of the plot and to pan around to examine different portions of the data.

- Clicking on the "**Arrows**" icon shown at "**4**" in **Figure 13-1** allows you to scroll through different pan and zoom settings that you have created.

- Clicking on the "**Home**" icon shown at "**5**" in **Figure 13-1** returns the zoom and pan settings back to their original values.

I have used these interactive panels to annotate and modify the original plot. The result is shown below.

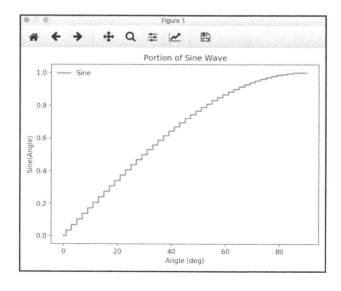

You can plot multiple curves on a single plot by executing a plot() command for each curve:

> julia> plot(Angle, **Sine**)
> julia> plot(Angle,**Cosine**)

The result, after some annotation, is shown below.

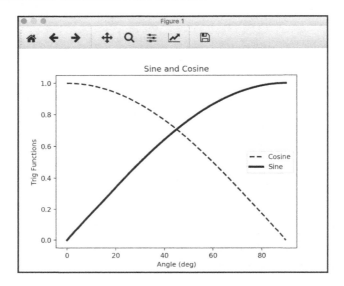

Although the interactive mode is useful for exploring data, it is unlikely that you would want to do all of the sizing and annotating by hand for every plot. Fortunately, with PyPlot you can produce a fully annotated plot ready for publication by making use of PyPlot keyword arguments

13.4 - Plotting Using the REPL

PyPlot provides functions and statements that allow you to generate and customize your plot using code rather than interactively.

The first step is to define the range and increment for the x and y axis grids:

> julia> xMin = 0.0;   # the value at the left end of the x-axis
> julia> xMax = 90.0;   # the value at the right end of the x-axis
> julia> dX   = 5.0;   # the increment between x-axis tic marks
>
> julia> yMin = 0.0;   # the value at the bottom end of the y-axis
> julia> yMax = 1.0;   # the value at the top end of the y-axis
> julia> dY   = 0.1;   # the increment between y-axis tic marks

All of these statements end with a semicolon to suppress inline output.

```
julia> xlim(xMin,xMax);        # these two PyPlot statements set the limits
julia> xticks(xMin:dX:xMax);   # and values for the x-axis ticks

julia> ylim(yMin,yMax);        # these two PyPlot statements set the limits
julia> yticks(yMin:dY:yMax);   # and values for the y-axis ticks

julia> title("Sine and Cosine") # define the title for the plot
julia> xlabel("Angle (°)");     # define the label for the x-axis
julia> ylabel("Trig Functions") # define the label for the y-axis

julia> plot(Angle,Sine,         # plot Sine vs Angle
            linewidth=3.0,      # set linewidth to 3.0 points
            color="red",        # set curve color to "red"
            label="Sine");      # set the name of the curve to "Sine"
julia> plot(Angle,Cosine,       # plot Cosine vs Angle
            linewidth=1.0,      # set linewidth to 1.0 points
            linestyle="--",     # set linestyle to dashed ("--")
            color="blue",       # set curve color to "blue"
            label="Cosine");    # set name of the curve to "Cosine"

julia> legend(loc="lower center");     # set the location of the legend

julia> tick_params(direction="in");    # set direction for the axis tick marks
julia> grid(linewidth=0.5,             # set grid line width = 0.5 points
            color="black",             # set grid line color to black
            linestyle="dotted",        # set grid line style to dotted
            alpha=0.5);                # set grid line transparency to 50%
```

As you enter each of these statements you will see the plot update in real time. The result of entering the statements above is the plot shown below.

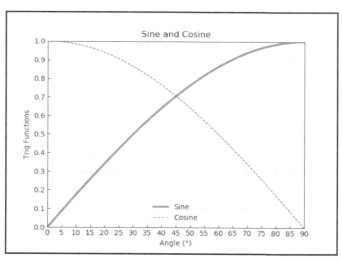

There are PyPlot keyword arguments such as "linewidth=1.0" that allow you to customize your plot and they will be described throughout this chapter.

13.5 - Plotting in the Jupyter Notebook

After a few trials it will become obvious that it is a lot of work to correct errors using the REPL. For serious plotting it is better to use the Jupyter Notebook environment where your code persists. For example, here is the Notebook equivalent of the REPL code shown on the previous page:

```
01   using Pkg                           # notice the Notebook syntax
02   Pkg.add("PyPlot")                    # notice the Notebook syntax
03   using PyPlot                         # notice the Notebook syntax
04   #-------------------------------
05   # generate the data
06   #-------------------------------
07   Angle  = collect(0.0:2.0:90.0)   # array of angles in degrees
08   Sine   = [sind(angle) for angle in Angle]
09   Cosine = [cosd(angle) for angle in Angle];
10   #-------------------------------
11   # plot the data
12   #-------------------------------
13   xMin  = 0.0
14   xMax = 90.0
15   dX    = 5.0
16   yMin  = 0.0
17   yMax  = 1.0
18   dY    = 0.1
19
20   figure(figsize=(8.0,5.75),dpi=200)
21   xlim(xMin,xMax)
22   xticks(xMin:dX:xMax)
23   ylim(yMin, yMax)
24   yticks(yMin:dY:yMax)
25   title("Portions of Sine & Cosine Wave")
26   xlabel("Angle (°)")
27   ylabel("Sine & Cosine (Angle)")
28   tick_params(direction="in")
29   grid(linewidth=0.5,color="black",linestyle="dotted",alpha=0.5)
30
31   plot(Angle,Sine,linewidth=3.0, label="Sine", color="red")
32   plot(Angle,Cosine,"--",linewidth=1.0,label="Cosine",
33   color="blue")
34
35   legend(loc="upper center")
36   show()
```

- line 01: using **Pkg** - the Julia package manager is **P**kg in the Jupyter Notebook and **p**kg in the REPL
- line02: Pkg.add("**PyPlot**") - the Notebook uses a different syntax than the REPL
- line 20: **figure**(figsize=(8.0,5.75),dpi=200) sets the plot size in inches and the raster resolution to 200 dpi (dots per inch).
- line 31: **linewidth**=3.0 sets the line width to 3 points (1 point = 1/72 inch)
- line 31: **label** is the name of the curve in the legend
- line 32: "--" specifies that the line should be dashed
- line 35: **legend**(loc="upper center") defines the location of the legend

These are known as keyword arguments for the various PyPlot functions and there are many, many of them. The result of this code is shown here:

Once you have generated the plot you want, the next step is to save it.

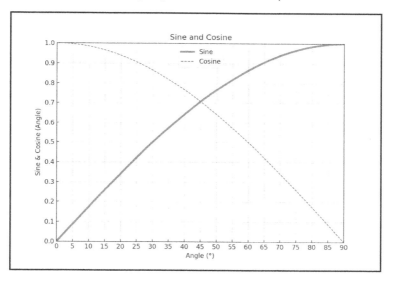

13.6 - Saving Plots

There are two ways to save a plot using the Jupyter Notebook:

1. Click anywhere in the plot and a menu box will pop-up. One of the options is "Save Image As...". Select this item and a dialog box will open allowing you to pick a save location and file name. Plots saved this way will have a .png file extension. Png (Portable Network Graphics) is a common format for saving "raster" images. Raster images save the data as an array of pixels, each with its own color and intensity. Raster image files are large - they basically store a photo

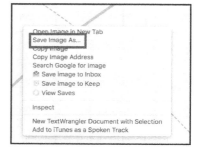

145

of the image. Raster images can also be of low resolution making them appear blurry if blown up too large. In the previous code fragment, line 20: **figure**(figsize=(8.0,5.75),dpi=200) set the size of the plot frame and also the resolution of the raster image. In this case the resolution is set at 200 dpi (dots or pixels per inch).making the raster image size 1600 x 1150 pixels = 1.8 Mpixels.

2. There is an automatic way to save your plot by including a savefig() function call in your code. To make this happen include these two statements at the end of your code

```
01      show()
02      PyPlot.savefig("myFile.png")
```

line01: The show() function displays the final plot in the Jupyter Notebook. It is important that the show() function call precedes the savefig() function call to avoid problems with the saved file.

line 02 The savefig() function is the one that saves your plot image to an external file. The file name extension you use to name the file determines what format is used to save the image. A file extension of .png saves the file in png (raster) format. Since png is the file format default, it is not necessary to include .png in the name you choose. For example savefig("myFile") would save your plot to a file named myFile.png in your working directory. Png is the only raster format available.

A file name extension of .svg (Scalable Vector Graphics) saves the plot in vector graphics format. These files are smaller than raster files and the plot image will appear sharp no matter how much it is enlarged. If you will save your plots as .svg files, there is no need to specify the dpi keyword in the call to **figure**(figsize=(width, height)).

Although svg is a better file format to use, some apps such as Adobe InDesign - the app I am using to write this book - cannot handle svg files. So, all of the examples in this book will save plots as .png files.

13.7 - Need for "PyPlot" in Function Calls

You may have noticed that the call to the savefig() function in line 02 above includes the "PyPlot" prefix. Why is that? There are two possible reasons that will require you to provide a prefix to your plot function calls:

1. PyPlot is based on the Python Matplotlib collection of plotting functions. But not all of these function names have been "exported" - that is they have not been made visible to Julia code. In this case you can still call the function but you have to use the complete function name which in this case is PyPlot.savefig().

2. There are several different plotting packages available for use in Julia. PyPlot is one of them. But PyPlot does not include every plotting function that is available. For example, PyPlot does not include the "bounding box" (bbox()) function that is needed for text plotting as will be described later. There is another plotting package, "StatPlots", that can be added to Julia. But, if you add the StatPlots package, that will create a name collision

because both PyPlot and StatPlots contain a function named savefig(). To resolve this name collision it is required to specify which function you want to call. Calling **PyPlot**.savefig() solves this problem. There are other name collisions that will require the PyPlot prefix. Calling one of these functions without the PyPlot prefix will throw an error.

13.8 - Line and Marker Styles

There are many keyword arguments that allow you to modify the default appearance of your plot. This code and the figure on the next page demonstrate some of them:

```
01  plot(x,y4,label="y4",              # set label of this line to "y4"
02      linewidth=0,                   # no line will be plotted
03      marker="*",                    # set markers to "star"
04      markersize=12,                 # set marker size to 12 points
05      markerfacecolor="red",         # color of marker interior = red
06      markeredgecolor="black")       # marker outline = black
07  plot(x,y3,label="y3",              # label of this line = "y3"
08      linewidth=1.5,                 # set linewidth to 1.5 points
09      linestyle="dashdot",           # set line style = dashdot
10      marker="^",                    # set marker to triangle
11      markersize=8,                  # set marker size = 8 points
12      markevery=2,                   # mark every 2nd plotted point
13      color="black")                 # color of the line = black
14  plot(x,y2,label="y2",              # label of this line = "y2"
15      linewidth=1.0,                 # set linewidth to 1.0 points
16      linestyle="dotted",            # set line style to dotted
17      marker="o",                    # set markers to small circles
18      markersize=8,                  # set marker size = 8 points
19      color="black")                 # color of the line = black
20  plot(x,y1,label="y1",              # label of this line = "y1"
21      linewidth=2.0,                 # set line width to 2.0 points
22      linestyle="solid",             # set line style to solid line
23      color="blue",                  # color of the line = blue
24      marker="o",                    # markers = small circles
25      markersize=12,                 # marker size = 12 points
26      markeredgecolor="black",       # color of marker edge = black
27      markerfacecolor="white")       # marker interior = white
```

The result of the previous code is shown below:

Note that the top line (y4) which was plotted with linewidth=0 shows only the markers. This is an easy way to generate a **scatter plot**.

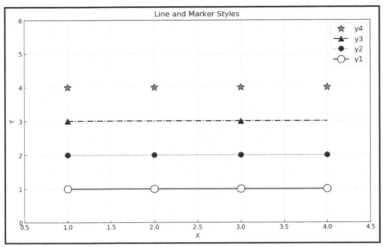

Line Styles:

- solid line   = **"solid"**   = "-" (one hyphen)
- dashed line   = **"dashed"**   = "--" (two hyphens)
- dash-dot line = **"dashdot"** = "-." (hyphen period)
- dotted line   = **"dotted"**   = ":" (colon)
- no line   = **"none"**   = " " (**space**) or linewidth=0

Marker Styles:

- "**.**" period => point
- "**,**" comma => pixel
- "**o**" (lowercase o) => circle
- "**v**" (lower case v) => triangle down
- "**^**" (upper case 6) => triangle up
- "**<**" => triangle left
- "**>**" => triangle right
- "**s**" => square
- "*****" => star
- "**+**" => plus sign
- "**x**" => x
- "**D**" => diamond
- "**l**" => vertical line
- and many more - refer to Julia documentation

Colors:

Julia supports essentially all color systems and a complete discussion would occupy this entire book. It is also difficult to discuss colors in black and white text. For a more complete discussion of Julia colors, refer to:

http://juliagraphics.github.io/Colors.jl/stable/index.html

http://juliagraphics.github.io/ColorSchemes.jl/stable/

For our introductory purposes, a basic color list will suffice:

- black = "**k**"
- blue = "**b**"
- cyan = "**c**"
- green = "**g**"
- magenta = "**m**"
- red = "**r**"
- white = "**w**"
- yellow = "**y**"

You can use the full name or the abbreviation. You can combine the color name abbreviations given above and the abbreviations for line styles and markers from the previous page. For example "**b--**" is a blue dashed line and "**ro-**" is a solid red line with circle markers.

You can also specify a named color other than those listed above. For example "beige" and "orchid" are named colors that Julia will recognize. The X11 named color list is common on Windows systems. For information on the X11 named color list goto: https://en.wikipedia.org/wiki/X11_color_names

In Julia the default color is black. When plotting multiple lines, Julia will choose black for the first line plotted and will then automatically cycle through a list of colors if you do not specify the colors you want.

More Keyword Arguments

We have already described several key words used when plotting lines and markers. Some keywords have abbreviations that make code more compact but harder to read. Here is a summary of the most useful keywords:

- **alpha** = transparency (0= transparent, 1= opaque)
- **color** = "c" = color definition or name
- **dashes** = custom sequence of ink on/off locations in points
- **drawstyle** = "default", "steps", "steps-pre", steps-mid", "steps-post"
- **label** = any printable string
- **linestyle** = ls = "solid", "dashed", "dashdot", "dotted" = "-", "--", "-.", ":"
- **linewidth** = lw = width of line in points
- **marker** = one of the previously described marker abbreviations
- **markeredgecolor** = mec = marker outline color
- **markerfacecolor** = mfc = marker fill color
- **markeredgewidth** = mew = width (points) of marker outline

- **markersize** = ms = marker size in points
- **markevery** = plot every nth marker
- **zorder** = 1 = lowest layer, 2 = next lowest, ..., big Int = frontmost

We have already seen most of these in action. Here is an example of the **drawstyle="steps"** keyword:

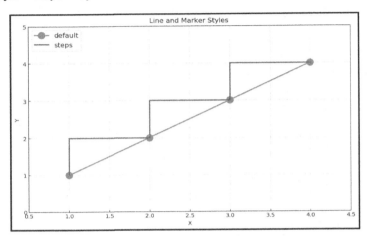

Here is an example of **alpha**, and plot functions **axvspan**, and **axhspan**:

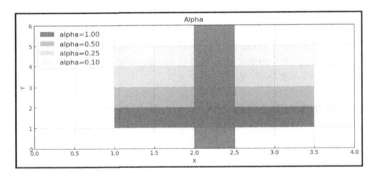

Here is the code that generated this figure:

```
01  axvspan(xmin=2.0, xmax=2.5,              # plots the vertical bar
02        color="black", alpha=0.5)
03  axhspan(ymin=1.0, ymax=2.0, xmin=0.25,
04        xmax=0.875, alpha=1.0, label="alpha=1.00")
05  axhspan(ymin=2.0, ymax=3.0, xmin=0.25,
06        xmax=0.875, alpha=0.5, label="alpha=0.50")
07  axhspan(ymin=3.0, ymax=4.0, xmin=0.25,
08        xmax=0.875, alpha=0.25,label="alpha=0.25")
09  axhspan(ymin=4.0, ymax=5.0, xmin=0.25,
10        xmax=0.875, alpha=0.1, label="alpha=0.10")
```

Plot function **axhspan**(ymin,ymax,xmin,xmax, ...) plots a horizontal bar from ymin to ymax in y-axis coordinates. The horizontal extent of this bar goes from xmin to xmax, but xmin and xmax are not in x-axis coordinates. xmin and xmax are specified as fractions of the x-axis length. So, in this case xmin = 1.0/4.0 = 0.25 and xmax = 3.5/4.0 = 0.875. If xmin and xmax are not specified they will default to xmin=0.0 and xmax = 1.0, that is, the bar will extend all the way across the plot.

The horizontal rectangular area is filled with the specified color and the specified alpha. Remember that alpha=0.0 makes the filled area transparent, alpha =1.0 makes the filled area opaque. You can see this in the figure on the previous page because of the vertical bar in the middle of the figure. This bar was plotted by the function **axvspan**() before any of the horizontal bars were drawn. This puts the vertical bar "behind" the horizontal bars. You can control which objects are "behind" others using the "**zorder**=..." keyword argument.

Here is an example of using the keyword "zorder" to move a plot object to the front of the layers:

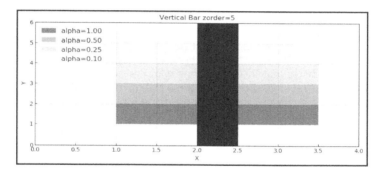

The vertical black bar was moved to the front of the plot using the zorder keyword:

01   axvspan(xmin=2.0, xmax=2.5, color="black", alpha=1.0, **zorder=5**)

This is the same code as used for the previous figure except that the vertical bar has been assigned **zorder=5** making it the front most object even though the plot code plots it first. Unless specified, zorder is assigned in the order of the plot() commands so the first curve plotted gets zorder=1. The next gets zorder=2, and so forth.

13.9 - Plotting Text and Annotations

It is often desired to add text and annotations to plots. Julia provides three functions to accomplish this:

- **text**() places text at a specified location on the plot
- **annotate**() places text and an arrow to point out a feature in the plot
- **arrow**() places an arrow (without text) on the plot

The first thing to do is to add the necessary plotting packages. For the following examples we need to add two plotting packages:

```
01  using Pkg                 # notice the Notebook syntax
02  Pkg.add("PyPlot")         # notice the Notebook syntax
03  using PyPlot              # notice the Notebook syntax
04  Pkg.add("StatPlots")     # StatPlots contains the bbox() function
05  using StatPlots          # StatPlots contains the bbox() function
```

Most of the plot functions we will use are in the PyPlot package. However, for the following examples, a second plot package, StatPlots, is required. StatPlots contains the bbox() function that will be used in these examples. Unfortunately, StatPlots contains at leat three functions with the same names used by PyPlot: text(), grid(), and savefig(). For this reason it is required to prepend the name of the package to the names of these duplicate named functions: PyPlot.text(), PyPlot. grid() and PyPlot.savefig().

13.9.1 - Plotting Text

This figure illustrates examples of text plotted using PyPlot.text() and many of its keywords:.

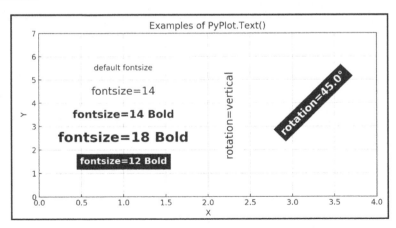

The code that generated this figure is listed on the following page.

You can identify which code produced which text example because the displayed text is included in the PyPlot.text() function call:

```
01  PyPlot.text(1.0,5.5, "default fontsize",
02      horizontalalignment="center",
03      verticalalignment="center",
04      bbox=Dict("color"=>"white"))
05  PyPlot.text(2.25,3.5, "rotation=vertical",
06      fontsize = 14.0,
07      horizontalalignment="center",
08      verticalalignment="center",
09      rotation="vertical",
10      bbox=Dict("color"=>"white"))
11  PyPlot.text(1.0,4.5, "fontsize=14",
12      fontsize = 14.0,
13      horizontalalignment="center",
14      verticalalignment="center",
15      bbox=Dict("color"=>"white"))
16  PyPlot.text(1.0,3.5, "fontsize=14 Bold",
17      fontsize = 14.0,
18      fontweight = "bold",
19      horizontalalignment="center",
20      verticalalignment="center",
21      bbox=Dict("color"=>"white"))
22  PyPlot.text(1.0,2.5, "fontsize=18 Bold",
23      fontsize = 18.0,
24      fontweight = "bold",
25      color="black",
26      horizontalalignment="center",
27      verticalalignment="center",
28      bbox=Dict("color"=>"white"))
29  PyPlot.text(1.0,1.5, "fontsize=12 Bold",
30      fontsize = 12.0,
31      fontweight = "bold",
32      color="white",
33      horizontalalignment="center",
34      verticalalignment="center",
35      bbox=Dict("color"=>"black"))
36  PyPlot.text(3.25,4.0, "rotation=45.0°",
37      fontsize = 14.0,
38      fontweight = "bold",
39      color="white",
40      rotation=45.0,
41      horizontalalignment="center",
```

```
42      verticalalignment="center",
43      bbox=Dict("color"=>"black"))
44  show()
```

The syntax of the PyPlot.text() function is:

PyPlot.text(x,y,"the text", kwargs...)

By default x,y are the x,y coordinates of the lower-left corner of the text frame in data coordinates. However this location will be modified if the keywords horizontalalignment (ha) and verticalalignment.(va) are given.

- **horizontalalignment = ha =** options are: :left", "right", and "center"
- **verticalalignment = va =** options are "top", "bottom", and "center"

  The actual x,y coordinate is located at the specified position on the text itself. So, "upper left" corresponds to the upper left corner of the text. This figure illustrates these options.

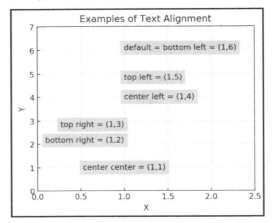

- **fontsize** (in points)
- **fontweight** options are: "normal","bold", "semibold", and "light"
- **fontstyle** options are: "normal", "italic"

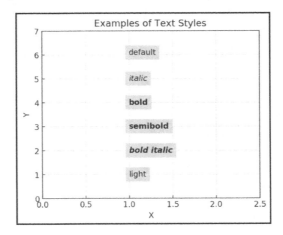

Which text options are actually available depends upon the chosen font. You can only specify a style actually offered by the font. The default for both the fontweight and fontstyle keywords is "normal".

- **bbox=Dict**("color"=>"white")

    The bbox() keyword draws a "bounding box" behind the text. By choosing a bbox() with a color of "white", distracting background objects are "erased" behind the text as illustrated in these examples:

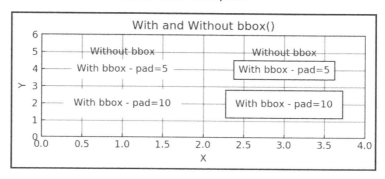

These examples were plotted with the following code fragments. We have discussed the text properties previously. What is new here is that a "bounding box" (bbox) has been added to the plot. A "bbox" is a rectangular area behind the text that can be assigned properties with a keyword argument list. In this case, the argument list is contained in a Dict (dictionary) of keyword=>value pairs.

This code plots a bounding box **without** an outline:

```
01   PyPlot.text(1.0,4.0, "With bbox - pad=5",
02       horizontalalignment="center",
03       verticalalignment="center",
04       bbox=Dict("color"=>"white","pad"=>5))
```

- "**color**" => any color. By picking "**color**" to be the same as the plot background color, generally white, plot objects between the text and the background will "disappear" as shown in the previous figure. Specifying "**color**" produces a bounding box **without** an outline.

- "**facecolor**" => any color In this case the keyword "color" has been replaced with the keyword "**facecolor**". This produces a bbox with an outline as shown in the examples on the right in the previous figure.

    This code plots a bounding box **with** an outline:

```
01   PyPlot.text(3.0,4.0, "With bbox - pad=5",
02       horizontalalignment="center",
03       verticalalignment="center",
04       bbox=Dict("facecolor"=>"white","pad"=>5))
```

- "**pad**"=>pixels. Specifies the padding around the text. The larger the padding, the larger the bounding box.

155

13.9.2 - Annotations

An "annotation" is a combination of some text and an arrow linked to that text. Some examples are shown in this figure:

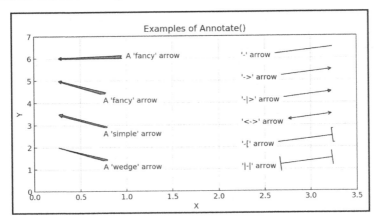

The code that produced this figure is:

```
01  annotate("A 'fancy' arrow", xy=(0.25,6.0), xytext=(1.0,6.0),
02          arrowprops=Dict("arrowstyle"=>"fancy"),
03          bbox=Dict("color"=>"white"))
04  annotate("A 'fancy' arrow", xy=(0.25,5.0), xytext=(0.75,4.0),
05          arrowprops=Dict("arrowstyle"=>"fancy"),
06          bbox=Dict("color"=>"white"))
07  annotate("A 'simple' arrow", xy=(0.25,3.5), xytext=(0.75,2.5),
08          arrowprops=Dict("arrowstyle"=>"simple"),
09          bbox=Dict("color"=>"white"))
10  annotate("A 'wedge' arrow", xy=(0.25,2.0), xytext=(0.75,1.0),
11          arrowprops=Dict("arrowstyle"=>"wedge"),
12          bbox=Dict("color"=>"white"))
13
14  annotate("'-' arrow",xy=(3.25,6.0),xytext=(2.25,5.5),
15          arrowprops=Dict("arrowstyle"=>"-"),
16          bbox=Dict("color"=>"white"))
17  annotate("'->' arrow",xy=(3.25,5.0),xytext=(2.25,4.5),
18          arrowprops=Dict("arrowstyle"=>"->"),
19          bbox=Dict("color"=>"white"))
20  annotate("'-|>' arrow",xy=(3.25,4.0),xytext=(2.25,3.5),
21          arrowprops=Dict("arrowstyle"=>"-|>"),
22          bbox=Dict("color"=>"white"))
23  annotate("'<->' arrow",xy=(3.25,3.0),xytext=(2.25,2.5),
24          arrowprops=Dict("arrowstyle"=>"<->"),
25          bbox=Dict("color"=>"white"))
```

```
26   annotate("'-[' arrow",xy=(3.25,2.0),xytext=(2.25,1.5),
27         arrowprops=Dict("arrowstyle"=>"-["),
28         bbox=Dict("color"=>"white"))
29   annotate("'I-I' arrow",xy=(3.25,1.0),xytext=(2.25,0.5),
30         arrowprops=Dict("arrowstyle"=>"I-I"),
31         bbox=Dict("color"=>"white"))
```

There are two different sets of arrows available. The first set contains three "fancy" arrows shown in the figure on the left side and in code lines 01 to 12. The second set of arrows is more simple and is illustrated on the right side of the figure and in code lines 14 to 31.

All annotate functions have two parameters: **xy** and **xytext**.

- **xy** = data coord of the tip of the arrow

- **xytext** = data coord of the text. By default this corresponds to the lower-left corner of the text but that can be changed using the horizontal and vertical alignment keywords as has been described previously. The text end (tail) of the arrow is computed by the annotate function and does not correspond to either of the xy coordinates given. It is not possible to directly control the coordinates of the tail of the arrow. This is unfortunate because the bbox needed to suppress plot items behind the text can interfere slightly with the tail end of the arrow as is visible in the figure for the "fancy", "simple", and "wedge" arrows.

- **arrowprops** controls which arrow type gets plotted. The **"arrowstyle"** key is contained in a dictionary (Dict) as illustrated in code lines 02, 05, 08, and 11 for the "fancy" arrows and in code lines 15, 21, 24, 27, and 30 for the simple arrows. For example line 15: **arrowprops**=Dict(**"arrowstyle"**=>"->") where the text "->" defines the arrow type. For arrows pointing in the opposite direction, reverse the characters in the arrowstyle value: "**->**" points right while "**<-**" points left.

Note: The arrowstyle "-" draws a line without an arrow head. If the annotation text is given as "", then no text is plotted but the arrow is. This is a good way to get just an arrow without the annotation text. There is a separate function **arrow**() that produces an arrow without text, but those arrows only "look good" it they are vertical or horizontal. At other angles the arrow heads are distorted. It is recommended that to produce an arrow you use annotate() without any text.

Annotate Connection Styles

It is possible to produce arrows with curved "shafts". This is accomplished by using the **connectionstyle** key in the arrowprops Dictionary. There are three connection style values that appear to work: "**arc3**, **angle3**, and **angle**. The code on the next page illustrates use of these key values and the figure on the page after that shows the results of the code. Connection styles "**angle**" and "**angle3**" take no parameters (that work). The **arc3** connection style does take one parameter (that works) **rad** presumably for radius but I have found no documentation for this. Basically, try values until you find one that looks the way you want it to. I have shown examples for rad=+0.25 (**arc3-01**), for rad=-0.25 (**arc3-02**) and for rad=-0.35 (**arc3-03**) to give an idea of the effect of variation in that parameter value. Once again experiment until you find a suitable value.

Example code to illustrate the connectionstyle key word:

```
01   annotate("(arc3-01)",xy=(1.25,6.0),xytext=(0.5,5.0),
02          verticalalignment="center",
03          horizontalalignment="center",
04          arrowprops=Dict("arrowstyle"=>"->",
05          "connectionstyle" => "arc3, rad=0.25"),
06          bbox=Dict("color"=>"white"))
07
08   annotate("(arc3-02)",xy=(1.0,4.0),xytext=(0.5,3.0),
09          horizontalalignment="center",
10          verticalalignment="center",
11          arrowprops=Dict("arrowstyle"=>"->",
12          "connectionstyle" => "arc3,rad=-0.25"),
13          bbox=Dict("color"=>"white"))
14
15   annotate("(arc3-03)",xy=(1.25,1.0),xytext=(0.5,2.0),
16          horizontalalignment="center",
17          verticalalignment="center",
18          arrowprops=Dict("arrowstyle"=>"->",
19          "connectionstyle" => "arc3,rad=-0.35"),
20          bbox=Dict("color"=>"white"))
21
22   annotate("(angle)",xy=(2.25,2.0),xytext=(1.75,1.0),
23          horizontalalignment="right",
24          verticalalignment="center",
25          arrowprops=Dict("arrowstyle"=>"->", "connectionstyle" => "angle"),
26          bbox=Dict("color"=>"white"))
27
28   annotate("(angle3-01)",xy=(2.25,6.0),xytext=(1.75,5.0),
29          horizontalalignment="center",
30          verticalalignment="center",
31          arrowprops=Dict("arrowstyle"=>"->", "connectionstyle" => "angle3"),
32          bbox=Dict("color"=>"white"))
33
34   annotate("(angle3-02)",xy=(1.5,4.0),xytext=(1.75,3.0),
35          horizontalalignment="left",
36          verticalalignment="center",
37          arrowprops=Dict("arrowstyle"=>"->", "connectionstyle" => "angle3"),
38          bbox=Dict("color"=>"white"))
```

The plot that results from this code is shown on the next page.

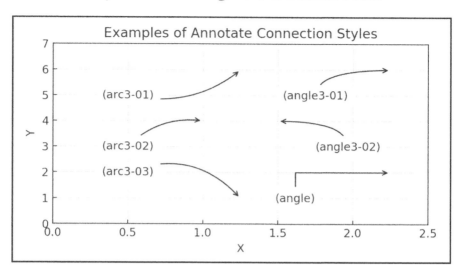

Annotate Arrow Styles

It is possible to modify the default appearance of the annotate arrow heads. Each arrow head style has associated parameters that will modify the size and length of the arrow head. Here are a few examples of arrow head modifications:

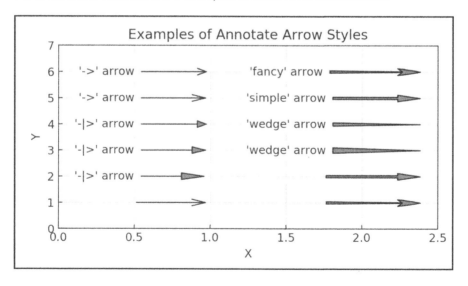

The code that produced this figure is on the next page. Notice that the bottom three arrows in the figure have no text associated with them. This is produced by setting the text string to "" (two double quotes) as is illustrated in lines 21, 43, and 46 in the code on the next page. You might be able to more easily produce the annotation you like by combining an arrow from annotate() and the text using the PyPlot.text function. That way you can move the text and arrow independently of one another.

Example code to illustrate modification of arrow head style:

```
01   annotate("'->' arrow",xy=(1.0,6.0),xytext=(0.5,6.0),
02         horizontalalignment="right", verticalalignment="center",
03         arrowprops=Dict("arrowstyle"=>"->, head_length=0.8, head_width=0.3"),
04         bbox=Dict("color"=>"white"))
05   annotate("'->' arrow",xy=(1.0,5.0),xytext=(0.5,5.0),
06         horizontalalignment="right", verticalalignment="center",
07         arrowprops=Dict("arrowstyle"=>"->, head_length=1.2, head_width=0.3"),
08         bbox=Dict("color"=>"white"))
09   annotate("'-I>' arrow",xy=(1.0,4.0),xytext=(0.5,4.0),
10         horizontalalignment="right", verticalalignment="center",
11         arrowprops=Dict("arrowstyle"=>"-I>, head_length=0.8, head_width=0.3"),
12         bbox=Dict("color"=>"white"))
13   annotate("'-I>' arrow",xy=(1.0,3.0),xytext=(0.5,3.0),
14         horizontalalignment="right", verticalalignment="center",
15         arrowprops=Dict("arrowstyle"=>"-I>, head_length=1.2, head_width=0.3"),
16         bbox=Dict("color"=>"white"))
17   annotate("'-I>' arrow",xy=(1.0,2.0),xytext=(0.5,2.0),
18         horizontalalignment="right", verticalalignment="center",
19         arrowprops=Dict("arrowstyle"=>"-I>, head_length=2.0, head_width=0.3"),
20         bbox=Dict("color"=>"white"))
21   annotate("",xy=(1.0,1.0),xytext=(0.5,1.0),
22         arrowprops=Dict("arrowstyle"=>"->, head_length=1.2, head_width=0.3"))
23   annotate("'fancy' arrow",xy=(2.4,6.0),xytext=(1.5,6.0),
24         horizontalalignment="center", verticalalignment="center",
25         arrowprops=Dict("arrowstyle"=>"fancy", head_length=2.0,
26         head_width=0.6,tail_width=0.2"),
27         bbox=Dict("color"=>"white"))
28   annotate("'simple' arrow",xy=(2.4,5.0),xytext=(1.5,5.0),
29         horizontalalignment="center",verticalalignment="center",
30         arrowprops=Dict("arrowstyle"=>"simple", head_length=2.0,
31         head_width=0.6"),
32         bbox=Dict("color"=>"white"))
33   annotate("'wedge' arrow",xy=(2.4,4.0),xytext=(1.5,4.0),
34         horizontalalignment="center",verticalalignment="center",
35         arrowprops=Dict("arrowstyle"=>"wedge", tail_width=0.3,
36         shrink_factor=0.5"),
37         bbox=Dict("color"=>"white"))
38   annotate("'wedge' arrow",xy=(2.4,3.0),xytext=(1.5,3.0),
39         horizontalalignment="center",verticalalignment="center",
40         arrowprops=Dict("arrowstyle"=>"wedge", tail_width=0.5,
41         shrink_factor=0.5"),
42         bbox=Dict("color"=>"white"))
```

```
43   annotate("",xy=(2.4,2.0),xytext=(1.75,2.0),
44        arrowprops=Dict("arrowstyle"=>"simple", head_length=2.0,
45        head_width=0.6"))
46   annotate("",xy=(2.4,1.0),xytext=(1.75,1.0),
47        arrowprops=Dict("arrowstyle"=>"fancy", head_length=2.0,
48        head_width=0.6, tail_width=0.2"))
```

So far we have been discussing line plots, but Julia provides techniques for producing other plot types. Some of these will be discussed in the following chapter.

Chapter 14

Other Types of Plots

Julia provides a number of different types of plots in addition to the simple line plots we have been discussing. I will discuss some of these in this chapter.

14.1 - Single Variable Plots

Typically we plot x vs y. But sometimes we have a single array of data that we want to visualize. Julia allows this by assuming that for y[i] the corresponding x[i]=i. This plots y[ ] vs the index number. For example:

```
01   using Pkg                    # notice the Notebook syntax
02   Pkg.add("PyPlot")            # notice the Notebook syntax
03   using PyPlot                  # notice the Notebook syntax
04
05   y  = collect(range(5;step=5,length=50))
06   plot(y,linewidth=2.0, color="blue")
07   show()
08   # let's try this:
09   i = 1
10   println(i,"   ",y[i])
```

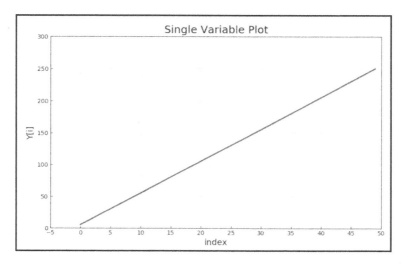

The printed output is:

```
1  5              # the value of y[1] at index=1 is 5
```

So, the listing shows the expected result that y[1] = 5, but a close look at the plot shows that the first point plotted is for index=0. In Julia there is no index=0. The single variable plot apparently reverts to Python where the index runs from 0 to 49. So, if you use a single variable plot, be aware that the plotted index values are 1 less than they are in Julia.

14.2 - Fill_Between Plots

In some situations it helps to visualize two data sets if you "fill between" them in a plot. For this Julia PyPlot provides the fill_between() function.

```
01  using PyPlot              # notice the Notebook syntax
02  -----------------
03  x  = collect(range(5;step=5,length=50))
04  y1 = 2*x
05  y2 = 3*x
06  -----------------
07  plot(x,y1,"--",linewidth=2.0,color="red")
08  plot(x,y2,"--",linewidth=2.0,color="red")
09  fill_between(x,y1,y2,color="blue", alpha=0.5)
10  show()
```

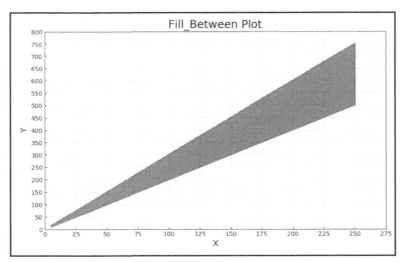

14.3 - Scatter Plots

As was mentioned previously, the easiest and fastest way to create a scatter plot is to use the standard line plot function plot() with markers and suppress the lines by setting linewidth=0:

```
01   using PyPlot
02   x  = collect(range(5;step=5,length=50))
03   y1 = 2.0*x
04   y2 = 2.5*x
05   y3 = 3.0*x
06   noise1 = 50*randn(50)
07   noise2 = 50*randn(50)
08   noise3 = 50*randn(50)
09   y1 = y1 + noise1
10   y2 = y2 + noise2
11   y3 = y3 + noise3
12   •••
13   plot(y1,y2, linewidth=0.0, color="blue", marker="s", label="Y2")
14   plot(y1,y3, linewidth=0.0, marker="o", markersize=8,
                 markeredgecolor="black", markerfacecolor="white",label="Y3")
15   legend(loc="upper left", fontsize="large")
16   show()
```

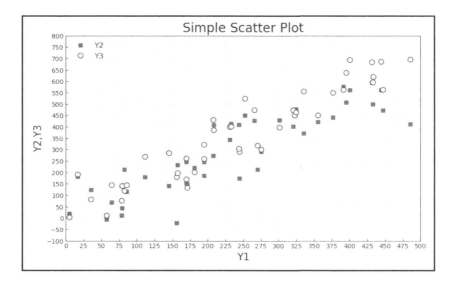

PyPlot also provides a dedicated function for plotting scatter plots: scatter(). Here are the lines of code that differ from those on the previous page:

13 PyPlot.scatter(y1,y2,facecolor="blue",marker="s",label="Y2")

14 PyPlot. scatter(y1,y3,facecolor="white",edgecolor="black",
        marker="o",s=64,label="Y3")

And here is the resulting scatter plot:

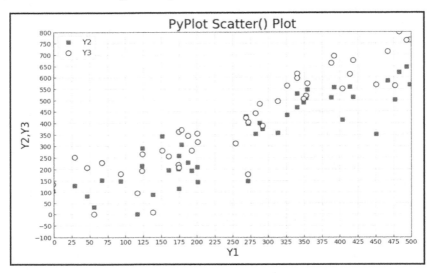

The result looks pretty much the same as for the simple line plot() scatter plot shown on the previous page. Note that the data are different because the random number generator was not seeded to the same value. This will be discussed in the chapter on Random Numbers

The PyPlot.scatter() function offers some capabilities such as using color sequences that are not available with plot(). But, if you don't need any of these capabilities, then using the simple plot() function to create a scatter plot is faster and easier to code because it uses the exact syntax as for plotting lines. Notice that the scatter() function uses a different syntax for some variables such as "s" for "markersize". Also note that the marker size is specified in some undefined units. The documentation says "points" but that is not correct. Just experiment until you find a value that you like.

14.4 - Histogram Plots

The Julia documentation provides several different ways of generating a histogram of data. For example, the documentation for the **"Distributions"** package describes a function named **"fit"**:

```
help?> fit                      # use REPL help to get info on fit
fit(Histogram, data)
Examples:
h = fit(Histogram, rand(100))   # the docs say this works
```

Let's see if it actually does work:

```
(v1.0) pkg> add Distributions
julia> using Distributions
julia> h=fit(Histogram,rand(100))
ERROR: UndefVarError: Histogram not defined    # it doesn't
```

Many of the other histogram functions either don't exist or don't work. Actually there is one that is part of the Plot package that does work - sort of.

```
help?> histogram
search: histogram histogram! histogram2d histogram2d!
No documentation found.
Plots.histogram is a Function.
```

So, even though "no documentation found", help?> did find that Plots.histogram is a function in the Plots package. Running this function in the REPL:

```
julia> Plots.histogram(data,bins=25)        # data = randn(500)
```

Results in this plot in a separate GKS Terminal window:

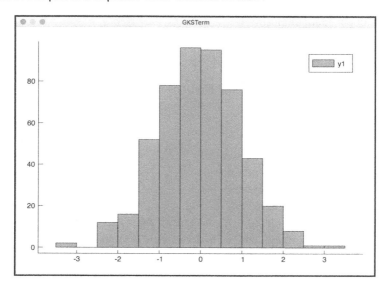

But, running the same code in the Jupyter Notebook environment results in nothing. No errors - no plot - nothing. Actually the function is probably running just fine but its output is still directed to a GKS terminal window instead of the Notebook. But, if all you want is a quick histogram plot and you can do that in the REPL, then Plot. histogram may be all you need.

Actually creating a histogram is so easy that there is little need to search through endless documents, as I have, trying to find something that works. Here's a quick function that plots a histogram of input data:

```
01  using Pkg
02  Pkg.add("PyPlot")
03  using PyPlot
04  #--------------------------------------------------
05  # define the plotHistogram function
06  #--------------------------------------------------
07  function plotHistogram(x, bins::Int)
08      minX  = minimum(x)
09      maxX = maximum(x)
10      span  = maxX-minX
11      binSize = span/numBins
12
13      binEdge = zeros(Float64,numBins+1)
14      binEdge[1] = minX
15      for index in 2:numBins+1
16          binEdge[index] = binEdge[index-1]+binSize
17      end # for index loop
18  # create the histogram
19      for i in 1:length(x)
20          global binCount
21          bin = (x[i]-minX)/binSize
22          intBin = 1+Int(trunc(bin))
23          binCount[intBin] = binCount[intBin]+1
24      end # for i loop
25  # Plot the histogram
26      figure(figsize=(10.0,6.0))
27      title("myHistogram", fontsize=18)
28      xlabel("Input Data", fontsize=14)
29      ylabel("Bin Count", fontsize=14)
30      tick_params(direction="in")
31      PyPlot.grid(linewidth=0.5, color="black", linestyle="dotted", alpha=0.5)
32      PyPlot.plot(binEdge, binCount, drawstyle="steps-post")
33      yTics = zeros(numBins+1)
34      PyPlot.plot(binEdge,yTics,linestyle="",marker="I",markersize=6
35      show()
```

Because we will need the histogram data later in Chapter 16 on optimization, we convert it to a DataFrame and then write that DataFrame to a text file using CSV. write():

```
36   df = DataFrame(bin=Int64[],binCenter=Float64[],binCount=Float64[])
37   for bin in 1:numBins+1
38       binCenter = (binSize/2.0) + binEdge[bin]
39       push!(df,[bin binCenter Float64(binCount[bin])])
40   end # bin loop
41   CSV.write("HistogramData.txt",df;delim='\t')
42   end #function plotHistogram
```

That's all there is to it. An example of using the **plotHistogram** function is shown below.

```
01   # ====================================
02   # setup some data
03   # ====================================
04   data     = randn(5000)
05   numBins  = 20
06   binCount = zeros(Int64,numBins+1)
07   plotHistogram(data,numBins)
```

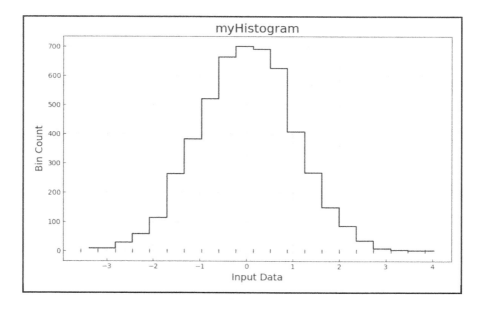

14.5 - LogLog and Semilog Plots

PyPlot has options for plotting on semilog and loglog axes. For example, here is a loglog plot:

```
using Pkg
Pkg.add("PyPlot")
using PyPlot

figure(figsize=(10.0,6.0))
title("Example of PyPlot.loglog", fontsize=18)
xlabel("X Data", fontsize=14)
ylabel("Y Data", fontsize=14)
tick_params(direction="in")
PyPlot.grid(linewidth=0.5, color="black", linestyle="dotted", alpha=0.5)

x = [1.0:100.0;]
y = [1.0:100.0;]

PyPlot.loglog(x,y, linewidth=3, color="black")

show()
```

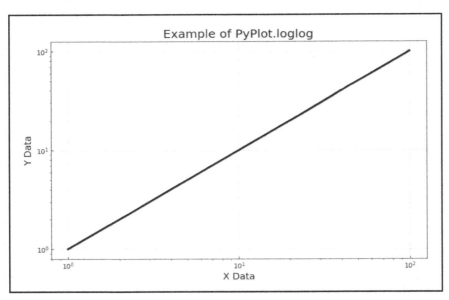

Here are the pertinent lines of code for a semi-log plots:

```
x = [1.0:100.0;]
y = [1.0:100.0;]
PyPlot.semilogx(x,y, linewidth=3, color="black")
```

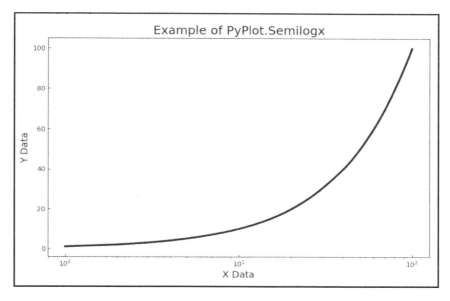

```
x = [1.0:100.0;]
y = [1.0:100.0;]
PyPlot.semilogy(x,y, linewidth=3, color="black")
```

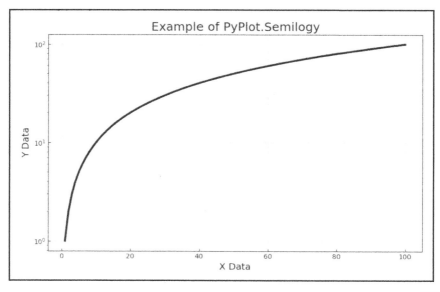

14.6 - Autocorrelation Plots

PyPlot provides a function that computes and then plots the autocorrelation function of input data. Here are the pertinent lines of code illustrating the auto correlation plot:

```
x = randn(100)
PyPlot.acorr(x, linewidth=3, color="black")
```

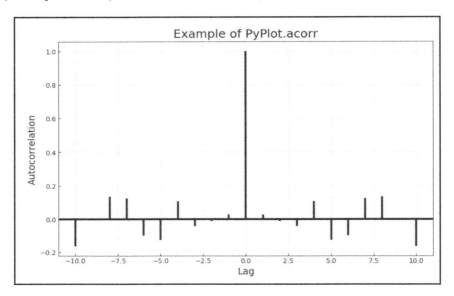

According to the documentation there is a matching PyPlot function for plotting the cross correlation between two arrays named xcorr(), but there is no such function in the Julia PyPlot package.

There are still many other types of plots that I will refer you to the documentation to learn about. Some are:

- bar plot - PyPlot.bar
- violin plot - PyPlot.violinplot
- contour plot - PyPlot.contour
- cross spectral density - PyPlot.csd
- pie chart - PyPlot.pie
- polar plot - PyPlot.polar
- power specral density - PyPlot.psd

and others

Chapter 15

Random Numbers

Julia provides a number of pseudo-random number generators. The default is the MersenneTwister generator. Others can be found in the package "RandomNumbers". The current random number generator is named "rng". In addition to the different generators, there are different packages that act as interfaces to the generators. Perhaps the easiest to use is cleverly named "Random". To install the "Random" package:

```
(v1.0) pkg> add Random
julia> using Random
```

15.1 - Seeding the Random Number Generator:

You can control the sequence of random numbers generated by "seeding" the RN generator. The same seed results in the same sequence of random numbers. This would be important if you want to compare the results of alternate ideas using the same sequence of random numbers.

There are two ways to seed the random number generator:

Seeding Method 1:

The first method selects the generator to use and the seed value to use. This statement selects the MersenneTwister algorithm and seeds it with the integer **1234**.

```
julia> rng = MersenneTwister(1234);  # note the semicolon
```

Having seeded rng we can generate a series of random numbers. The function randn() generates one or more normally distributed Float64 random numbers. The following statement uses the current rng to generate four random numbers:

```
julia> randn(rng,4)          # that the generator name "rng" is used
 0.8673472019512456
-0.9017438158568171
-0.4944787535042339
-0.9029142938652416
```

If we ask for four more numbers, we get a different sequence:

```
julia> randn(rng,4)
 2.2118774995743475
 0.5328132821695382
-0.27173539603462066
 0.5023344963886675
```

But if we re-seed the generator with the same seed, we get the original sequence of numbers:

> julia> rng = **MersenneTwister(1234);**

> julia> randn(rng,4)
>   0.8673472019512456
> -0.9017438158568171
> -0.4944787535042339
> -0.9029142938652416

Seeding Method 2:

If you want to use the default MersenneTwister generator, you can use a simpler syntax leaving out the rng name. The following statement uses the default rng, the MersenneTwister algorithm, and seeds it with the integer **1234**.

> julia> **Random.seed!(1234);**   # note the semicolon

Because the default rng is going to be used, it is not necessary to name it:

> julia> **randn**(4)
>   0.8673472019512456
> -0.9017438158568171
> -0.4944787535042339
> -0.9029142938652416

Notice that this is the same sequence generated by the previous statements.

15.2 - Suppressing Output

Generally you are going to want a series, perhaps a very long series, of random numbers and it would be inconvenient to have them all listed as in the examples above. Julia provides a couple of ways to suppress or at least shorten listed output. We have already seen one of these methods. Following any Julia statement with a semicolon (;) will suppress printing of any output that statement might produce.

Without a semicolon the results of the randn() function are listed:

> julia> x = randn(4)
>   0.8673472019512456
> -0.9017438158568171
> -0.4944787535042339
> -0.9029142938652416

The same statement followed by a semicolon is executed but no output is created.

> julia> x = randn(4);

Following a statement with a comma (,) does not suppress output, but it does present it in a more compact format:

> julia> x = randn(4),
>   ([0.502334, -0.516984, -0.560501, -0.0192918],)

Don't worry if you forget the semicolon after a statement like randn(10000). Julia will not list all 10,000 random numbers. Only a short section of the first and last portions of the entire array will be listed.

15.3 - Random Number Distributions

The Random package has three different random number distributions built in:

- **rand(n)** generates an array of "n" Float64 uniformly distributed random numbers on the interval 0-1:

  julia> **rand**(4)
  4-element Array{Float64,1}:
   0.06642303695533736
   0.9567533636029237
   0.646690981531646
   0.11248587118714015

- **randn(n)** generates an array of "n" Float64 "normally" distributed random numbers with mean=0.0 and standard deviation=1.0:

  julia> **randn**(4)
  4-element Array{Float64,1}:
   -0.2511757400198831
    0.3697140350317453
    0.07211635315125874
   -1.503429457351051

- **randexp(n)** generates an array of "n" Float64 "exponentially" distributed random numbers with scale=1:

  julia> **randexp**(4)
  4-element Array{Float64,1}:
   0.5658208511668084
   3.784459824738665
   1.8303409699363329
   2.6478748641888625

In all these cases an empty set of parentheses will generate a single random number.

15.4 - Other Random Distributions

Julia has a package that provides more random number distributions. This package is cleverly named "Distributions" and provides at least these distribution types.

- Bernoulli
- Beta
- Binomial
- Categorical
- DiscreteUniform
- Exponential
- Normal
- Gamma
- Geometric
- Laplace
- Pareto
- Poisson
- Uniform

For each of these distributions the package can generate a single or an array of random numbers drawn from that distribution or given a set of random numbers it can fit a specified distribution to that array of numbers.

Before you can use these distributions, you must add the Distributions package:

```
(v1.0) pkg> add Distributions
julia> using Distributions
```

With the package added, you can generate an array of random numbers drawn from one of the supported distributions.

```
julia> mean   = 2.5
julia> sigma  = 1.75
julia> number = 500
julia> rn = rand(Normal(mean,sigma), number);
```

When using the Distributions package, the random number generator is always named "rand" regardless of the actual distribution. In this example the **Normal** (Gaussian) distribution is used, You can specify the parameters of the distribution inside the parentheses as illustrated above for the mean and sigma of the Normal distribution. After this function call, the variable rn will contain "number" (500) random numbers drawn from a Normal distribution with the specified mean and sigma.

Given an array of random numbers, you can obtain an estimate of the distribution's parameters by calling the Distributions "**fit()**" function. You must specify the distribution for which the parameters will be estimated.

```
julia> a = fit(Normal,rn)
Normal{Float64}(μ=2.408280168678194, σ=1.7556017995231088)

julia> mean = params(a)[1]
2.408280168678194
julia> sigma = params(a)[2]
1.7556017995231088
```

The best fit parameters can be recovered using the syntax:

parameter value = params(fit)[i]

as illustrated in the example.

The **Beta** distribution is also handy. It frequently provides a good model of real observations where the values are limited to a finite range. Here's an example of generating an array of random numbers (rn) drawn from a **Beta**(2.0,2.0) distribution:

```
julia> a = 2.0
julia> b = 2.0
julia> rn = rand(Beta(a,b),5000)
```

Given the array of random numbers (rn) we can estimate the parameter of the Beta distribution using fit:

```
julia> dist = fit(Beta,x)
julia> a = params(dist)[1]
2.013472498746833
julia> b = params(dist)[2]
2.0399550116375247
```

Here is an example of the Beta distribution histogram and the best fit parameters:

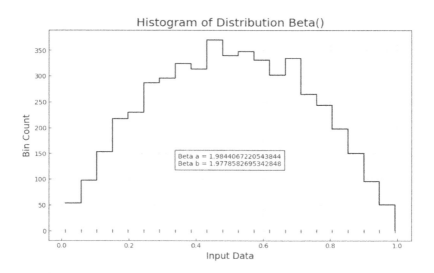

You can find out more about the Distributions package at:

https://juliastats.github.io/Distributions.jl/latest/index.html

and about the distributions themselves at

15.5 - Random Number Types

The package **Random** can generate random numbers of different Types. The default, as illustrated above, is Float64. If a type other than Float64 is desired, that Type can be specified in the function call:

```
julia> rand(Int64,4)          # generates uniformly distributed integers
4-element Array{Int64,1}:
  3760053215810934900
 -2306413346197920421
 -6433525651070979275
  6559438366294161292
```

The supported types are: Float16, Float32, Float64 (the default), and their Complex counterparts.

```
julia> rand(Float32,4)
4-element Array{Float32,1}:
 0.43502915
 0.39022183
 0.7691536
 0.71585083
```

Random can generate a random string of characters. The set of characters from which the result is drawn consists of upper and lower case letters and numbers.

```
julia> randstring(10)
"DRrRT760FY"
```

15.6 - Drawing From a Set

The function rand() can make random draws from a set of possibilities. The following statement draws 4 random selections from the range of integers 1:10:

```
julia> rand(1:10,4)
4-element Array{Int64,1}:
 4
 6
 9
 6
```

And this statement draws from a range of Floats:

```
julia> rand(1.0:0.25:10.0,4)
4-element Array{Float64,1}:
 2.25
 9.0
 7.25
 5.0
```

Randstring can generate a random string from a specified list of characters:

```
julia> randstring("abcdABCD",8)        # draw 8 characters from the set
"BbcAccdD"
```

15.7 - Random Number Arrays

One way to generate an array of random numbers has already been shown. Simply give the array a name and call rand() to create and fill the array.

```
julia> x = rand(4)
4-element Array{Float64,1}:
 0.7480405976865343
 0.265559536159694797
 0.29106864128858234
 0.6126276964747348
```

The array **x** now contains 4 uniformly distributed random numbers:

```
julia> x
4-element Array{Float64,1}:
 0.7480405976865343
 0.265559536159694797
 0.29106864128858234
 0.6126276964747348
```

Another approach is to define the array first and then fill it with random numbers. Each of the random number generating functions has a slightly different syntax to fill an already existing array:

```
julia> y = zeros(4)     # create an array
4-element Array{Float64,1}:
 0.0
 0.0
 0.0
 0.0

julia> rand!(y)         # to fill an existing array use the  ! syntax
4-element Array{Float64,1}:
 0.5083634348868193
 0.47255030550110577
 0.6125537989226799
 0.1926340924375769
```

There are similar **randn!**() and **randexp!**() functions that fill existing arrays

15.8 - Shuffle and Shuffle!

The shuffle() function returns a random permutation of the elements in an array:

```
julia> z = collect(4:7)        # generate the original array
4
5
6
7

julia> shuffle(z)              # shuffle the elements of the array
5
7
6
4
```

The original array (z) has not been modified so it is possible to loop around and generate a different permutation:

```
julia> z                       # the original array is not changed
4
5
6
7

julia> shuffle(z)              # generate a new shuffle of the array
7
4
6
5
```

You can also shuffle in place using the ! syntax if it is not necessary to save the original array:

```
julia> shuffle!(z)             # the ! syntax shuffles in place
6
4
5
7

julia> z                       # the array z has been shuffled
6
4
5
7
```

Chapter 16

Optimization

"Optimization" refers to the process of finding a set of variables that maximize some "benefit" or minimize some "cost" subject to constraints. A common example is finding a set of parameters that minimize the least squared difference between an analytic function and a set of measured data.

16.1 - Simple Linear Regression:

The simplest case of optimization is to find a linear fit to measured data. In earlier versions of Julia there used to be a function named linreg() that accomplished this task, but it has been removed in v1.0. Fortunately it is pretty simple to write your own function to solve this problem using the LinearAlgebra package.

```
01  # myLinReg
02  # Fit a simple linear expression: y = a*x + b
03  # ------------------------------------------------------
04  using Pkg
05  Pkg.add("LinearAlgebra")
06  using LinearAlgebra
07  # ------------------------------------------------------
08  function myLinReg(xData,yData)
09      num   = length(xData)
10      X     = zeros(num,2)
11      X[:,1] = xData
12      one   = ones(num)
13      X[:,2] = one
14      ab    = X\yData          # note the backslash
15      return ab
16  end
17  # ------------------------------------------------------
18  # generate some test data:
19  a  = 4.0
20  b  = 2.5
21  num = 100
22  xData = rand(num)
23  yTrue = a*xData .+ b
24  yData = yTrue + randn(num) * 0.5
```

```
25   ab = myLinReg(xData,yData)
26
27   println()
28   println("y = ax + b")
29   println("True a = ",a)
30   println("True b = ",b)
31   println("Estimated ab = ",ab)
32   # ----------------------------------------------
33   y = ax + b
34   True a = 4.0
35   True b = 2.5
36   Estimated ab = [3.89273, 2.53729]
```

The actual linear regression function occupies only 9 lines of code

For more complex curve fitting problems Julia provides the "Optim" package to handle this type of problem as the following example will illustrate.

16.2 - Example Using Solver "Optim":

Optim is a stand alone solver package that is ideal for finding a set of parameter values that result in an "optimum" fit between an analytic function and some measured data. Just such a problem is presented by the histogram plot example from section 14.4.

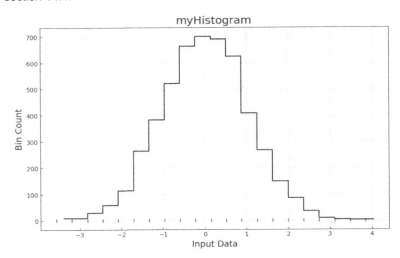

Because this histogram was created from random data generated by the randn() function, we expect that the histogram should be Gaussian. So let's try fitting the histogram data to a Gaussian function using the Optim package.

The code is shown on the following page.

```
01  using Pkg
02  Pkg.add("Optim")
03  using Optim
04  Pkg.add("DataFrames")
05  using DataFrames
06  Pkg.add("CSV")
07  using CSV
08  Pkg.add("Printf")
09  using Printf
10  Pkg.add("PyPlot")
11  using PyPlot

12  #-----------------------------------------------------------------------------------
13  # read the Histogram data from a DataFrame file
14  #-----------------------------------------------------------------------------------
15  df = CSV.read("HistogramData.txt";delim='\t')
16  xData   = df[:binCenter]
17  yData   = df[:binCount]
18  numBins = length(xData)

19  #-----------------------------------------------------------------------------------
20  # create a function that computes the squared error for parameters p[ ]
21  #-----------------------------------------------------------------------------------
22  p = zeros(3)  # p are the unknown parameters of the Gaussian
23  function f(p) # f(p) returns the squared error between data and Gaussian
24      sqerror = 0.0
25      for i in 1:length(xData)
26          est = p[1]*(exp(-(xData[i]-p[2])^2/(2.0*p[3]^2)))        # a Gaussian
27          sqerror = sqerror + (yData[i]-est)^2
28      end# for loop
29      return sqerror
30  end # function f(p)

31  result = optimize(f, [0.5,0.5,0.5])        # this minimizes the squared error

32  p1 = Optim.minimizer(result)[1]
33  p2 = Optim.minimizer(result)[2]
34  p3 = Optim.minimizer(result)[3]

35  println()
36  println("Optimum Fit Parameters:")
37  println("p1 = ",p1)
38  println("p2 = ",p2)
39  println("p3 = ",p3)
```

```
40  #-------------------------------------------------------------------------
41  # plot the histogram data
42  #-------------------------------------------------------------------------
43  PyPlot.figure(figsize=(10.0,6.0))
44  title("Optim Gaussian Example", fontsize=18)
45  xlabel("X", fontsize=14)
46  ylabel("Y", fontsize=14)
47  tick_params(direction="in")
48  PyPlot.grid(linewidth=0.5, color="black", linestyle="dotted", alpha=0.5)
49  PyPlot.plot(xData,yData,linewidth=1,drawstyle="steps-mid",color="black",
    label="Histogram")

50  #-------------------------------------------------------------------------
51  # plot the Gaussian fit
52  #-------------------------------------------------------------------------
53  x = collect(range(xData[1],stop=xData[end],length=41))
54  y = p1.*(exp.(-(x.-p2).^2/(2.0.*p3.^2)))
55  PyPlot.plot(x,y,"--", linewidth=1,color="black",label="Gaussian Fit")
56  legend(loc="upper left", fontsize="large")

57  #-------------------------------------------------------------------------
58  # annotate the plot
59  #-------------------------------------------------------------------------
60  str1 = @sprintf("Optim Fit Parameters\n\n")
61  str2 = @sprintf("Peak = %3.3f\n",p1)
62  str3 = @sprintf("Mean = %3.3f\n",p2)
63  str4 = @sprintf("Sigma = %3.3f",p3)
64  str5 = str1*str2*str3*str4

65  PyPlot.text(0.0,175.0, str5,
66      fontsize=12,
67      horizontalalignment="center",
68      verticalalignment="top",
69      bbox=Dict("color"=>"white","pad"=>5))

70  show()
```

The resulting plot is shown on the next page.

Optim Gaussian Example

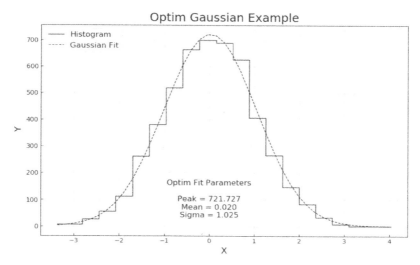

Optim Fit Parameters

Peak = 721.727
Mean = 0.020
Sigma = 1.025

Comments on the code:

- lines 04-11: These packages are only needed for reading, writing, and plotting the histogram data and can be omitted if those functions are not needed.

- lines 12-18: These lines read the histogram data from a CSV DataFrame file that was written back in section 14.4 where the histogram was created. Once again these lines can be omitted if the data to be fit are generated in the code where Optim is being executed.

- lines 19-30: This is the heart of the Optim code and is the reason that Optim is such a powerful tool. Optim is designed to optimize a function of parameters that the programmer can define external to the Optim code itself. This function can be any code that accepts a set of parameters and returns a measure of how well those parameters fit the measured data. In this case, as will be the typical case, the measure of "fitness" is the sum of the squares of the differences between the analytic function and the measured data but it can be anything the user wants.

- line 22: The parameters to be optimized are contained in an array "p[ ]"

- line 23: Notice that the function **f(p)** accepts only the parameter array as an argument. It is not necessary to include the measured data, xData and yData in this case, because those data are "constants" that do not change in the optimization process. They are "visible" to the function and need not be included as arguments. The only function of **f(p)** is to compute the "cost" resulting from that set of parameters.

- line 26: This line of code defines the analytic function of parameters "p" that is being matched to the measured data. This function can be as complex as needed to define the problem.

- line 31: This is the call to the Optim function "optimize()" that does all the work. Notice that the cost function f(p) is the first argument. The three element array [0.5,0.5,0.5] contains the initial guess at the parameter values. By default optimize() minimizes the cost function f(p). Including the keyword "Max" in the argument list will cause optimize() to choose parameter values that maximize the function f(p). The function optimize() accepts many other arguments and I direct your attention to the docs to read all about them.

- lines 32-34: Many of the docs describing optimization functions go to great lengths to tell you how to run the function but then neglect to tell you how to access the results. In the Optim case, the resulting "optimimum" parameter values are contained in an array called "Optim.minimizer(result)". As shown in the code, the parameters, p1, p2 and p3, are the elements in that array. There is a lot more information contained in the "result" of the optimize() function and once again the docs are your best resource for this information.

- lines 35-39: Print the optimum parameter values to the Notebook.

- lines 40-49: Plot the input histogram data. As with any plot created in the Jupyter Notebook, you can right-click on the plot and choose a name and place to store that plot. If you end the name with the extension ".png", the plot will be stored as a raterized png file. If you use the filename extension ".svg" the plot will be stored as a scaled vector graphics (not raterized) file.

- lines 50-56: Generate and plot the best fit Gaussian.

- lines 60-63: Use the macro @**sprintf()** to write the formatted parameter values to strings. I use separate @sprintf() staments for each parameter because it is easier to read and fits on the page better.

- line 64: Concatenates the strings str1 thru str4 intio a single string, str5, that can be passed to the PyPlot.text() function. Remember that for strings, the character '*' concatenates the strings. The results are shown in the plot on the previous page.

The **Optim** package is very powerful and is very easy to use as has been illustrated. But modern optimization problems can be much more complex than simple "curve fitting". Scheduling NFL football games so as to minimize team travel times and selecting the set of roads that will get you from "a" to "b" in the shortest time are two examples of optimization problems that cannot be solved using the same algorithms that work for simple parameter optimization problems. Julia provides another optimization package that reveals a wide range of "solver" functions suited to different types of problems. That package is called JuMP.

16.3 - Introduction to JuMP:

Julia provides a number of optimization engines and a user interface named "JuMP" that allows the user to define the optimization problem and calls the appropriate engine to solve it. In modern jargon "optimization" is more broadly defined as "**M**athematical **P**rogramming" and JuMP is the Julia package that handles a wide variety of mathematical programming problems. The JuMP structure is illustrated below:

JuMP itself is actually a user interface designed to permit an optimization problem to be defined in a common syntax regardless of problem type and which actual "solver" is to be used. At the time this book is being written, the JuMP interface calls the **MathProgBase** intermediate layer which in turns calls the actual solver. However, the **MathProgBase** is being updated and replaced by a new intermediate layer named **MathOptInterface** which is abbreviated as "**MOI**". This change in intermediate layer will most likely necessitate some changes to the JuMP user interface so some of the examples to be shown here may have to be modified once the switch over is finished.

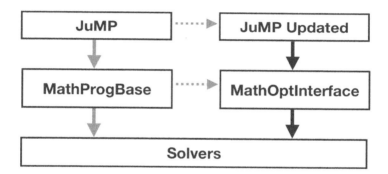

JuMP provides a consistent user interface regardless of problem type and solver selection. For a current list of available JuMP solvers goto:

http://www.juliaopt.org/

16.4 - JuMP Syntax

Model:

Every JuMP problem is associated with a model. The syntax for creating a model is:

- **myModel** = Model(solver=name of solver())

In some cases the solver specification can be omitted and JuMP will choose a solver based on the model description.

Variables:

Variables are defined using the macro @variable() which allows definition of the variable name and constraints on the range of possible variable values:

- @variable(myModel, **x**)
- @variable(myModel, **x >= lowerBound**)
- @variable(myModel, **x <= upperBound**)
- @variable(myModel, **lowerBound <= x <= upperBound**)

An initial value of the variable can be provided with the start= keyword

- @variable(myModel, 0.0<= x <=10.0,**start=5.0**)

Variables can be arrays

- @variable(myModel, **x[1:5]**)

Objective:

The objective of the model is to maximize (Max) or minimize (Min) some expression.

- @objective(myModel,Max or Min, some expression)

Constraints:

The solution may be subject to one or more constraints.

- @constraint(myModel, sum(x[i] for i=1:N >= 0.0)

Solving the Model:

The model is solved using the specified solver by:

- status=solve(myModel)

Getting the Results:

Each solver seems to have its own method for returning the results of the optimization process. The documentation is often not helpful in this matter and it is necessary to go to the source code to discover where the results have been hidden. In the following examples, I will show how to get the results for the solvers in the examples.

JuMP currently supports about a dozen different solver engines that handle different types of problems. I will illustrate examples for four of these solvers. Most of these examples have been taken directly from the JuMP documentation. My primary aim in showing these examples here is to make sure that they actually work as described in the docs and to provide a template that you can use to build your own solutions.

16.5 - Ipopt Example

Ipopt is one of the optimization solvers that can be called from JuMP. **Ipopt** can handle both linear and nonlinear models.

https://github.com/JuliaOpt/Ipopt.jl

Here is a very simple example using the Ipopt solver to solve a nonlinear problem:

```
01   using Pkg
02   Pkg.add("JuMP")
03   using JuMP
04   Pkg.add("Ipopt")
05   using Ipopt

06   m = Model(solver = IpoptSolver())

07   @variable(m, 0 <= x <= 2 )
08   @variable(m, 0 <= y <= 30 )

09   @objective(m, Min, x*x+ 2x*y + y*y )

10   @constraint(m, x + y >= 1 )
11   print(m)
12   status = solve(m)
13   println("Objective value: ", getobjectivevalue(m))
14   println("x = ", getvalue(x))
15   println("y = ", getvalue(y))
```

Ipopt provides a multitude of output information. The result of the print(model) command in line 11 is:

Min $x^2 + 2 x*y + y^2$

Subject to

$x + y \geq 1$

$0 \leq x \leq 2$

$0 \leq y \leq 30$

This is Ipopt version 3.12.10, running with linear solver mumps.
NOTE: Other linear solvers might be more efficient.

Number of nonzeros in equality constraint Jacobian	0
Number of nonzeros in inequality constraint Jacobian.	2
Number of nonzeros in Lagrangian Hessian	3
Total number of variables	2
variables with only lower bounds	0
variables with lower and upper bounds	2
variables with only upper bounds	0
Total number of equality constraints	0

Total number of inequality constraints.	1
inequality constraints with only lower bounds	1
inequality constraints with lower and upper bounds:	0
inequality constraints with only upper bounds:	0
Number of Iterations....	7

EXIT: Optimal Solution Found.

And finally the actual results printed by the print() statements in lines 13-15:

Objective value: 0.9999999825046585
x = 0.27864390938942063
y = 0.7213560818629086

16.6 - Clp Example

Clp (**C**oin-or **L**inear **P**rogramming) is an open-source linear programming solver. For more information refer to:

https://www.coin-or.org/Clp/userguide/index.html

Here is a simple example using the Clp solver:

```
01   using Pkg
02   Pkg.add("JuMP")
03   Pkg.add("Clp")
04   using JuMP
05   using Clp

06   m = Model(solver=ClpSolver())
07   @variable(m, 0<=x<=2)
08   @variable(m, 0<=y<=30)

09   @objective(m, Max, 5*x + 3*y)

10   @constraint(m, x + 5*y <=3.0)

11   print(m)

12   status = solve(m)

13   println("Objective value = ", getobjectivevalue(m))
14   println("x = ", getvalue(x))
15   println("y = ", getvalue(y))
```

The result of the print(m) command in line 11 is:

```
Max 5 x + 3 y
Subject to
 x + 5 y ≤ 3
 0 ≤ x ≤ 2
 0 ≤ y ≤ 30
```

190

The result of the println() commands in lines 13-15 are:

> Objective value = 10.6
> x = 2.0
> y = 0.2

16.7 - NLopt Example

As the name implies, the **NLopt** solver is designed for nonlinear problems. Both objective and constraints can be nonlinear functions.

```
01   using Pkg
02   Pkg.add("JuMP")
03   using JuMP
04   Pkg.add("NLopt")
05   using NLopt
06   m = Model(solver=NLoptSolver(algorithm=:LD_MMA))
07   a1 = 2
08   b1 = 0
09   a2 = -1
10   b2 = 1
11   @variable(m, x1)
12   @variable(m, x2 >= 0)
13   @NLobjective(m, Min, sqrt(x2))
14   @NLconstraint(m, x2 >= (a1*x1+b1)^3)
15   @NLconstraint(m, x2 >= (a2*x1+b2)^3)
16   setvalue(x1, 1.234)
17   setvalue(x2, 5.678)
18   status = solve(m)
19   println()
20   print(m)
21   println()
22   println("Optimum ", getobjectivevalue(m))
23   println("Found at x1 = ", getvalue(x1))
24   println("Found at x2 = ", getvalue(x2))
25   println()
```

The results of the print statements in lines 19-25 are:

> Min sqrt(x2)
> Subject to
> x2 - (2.0 * x1 + 0.0) ^ 3.0 ≥ 0
> x2 - (-1.0 * x1 + 1.0) ^ 3.0 ≥ 0
> x1
> x2 ≥ 0

Optimum 0.5443310477213124
Found at x1 = 0.3333333342139688
Found at x2 = 0.29629628951338166

16.8 - Cbc Example

The **Cbc** solver is designed for mixed integer problems where the variables and constraints can be integers. This example is a version of the knapsack problem that was presented by Philip Thomas on Jun 25, 2016 at the OpenLate Meetup Group about optimization in Julia using the JuMP package. The objective is to minimize the weight of coins needed to total 99 cents.

```
01   using Pkg
02   Pkg.add("JuMP")
03   Pkg.add("Cbc")
04   using JuMP
05   using Cbc
06   myModel = Model(solver=CbcSolver())
07   @variable(myModel,pennies >=0, Int)
08   @variable(myModel,nickels >=0, Int)
09   @variable(myModel,dimes   >=0, Int)
10   @variable(myModel,quarters >=0, Int)
11   # we want exactly 99 cents
12   @constraint(myModel,pennies+5*nickels+10*dimes+25*quarters == 99)
13   # we want to minimize weight. The numbers are the weights of each coin
14   @objective(myModel, Min, 2.5*pennies + 5.0*nickels + 2.268*dimes +
5.670*quarters)
15   println()
16   println("The Model to be Optimized:")
17   print(myModel)
18   # solve the problem
19   status = solve(myModel)
20   # get and print results:
21   println()
22   println("The Optimum Solution:")
23   println("Minimum Weight = ",getobjectivevalue(myModel)," grams")
24   println("Achieved with:")
25   println(Int(round(getvalue(pennies)))," pennies")
26   println(Int(round(getvalue(nickels)))," nickels")
27   println(Int(round(getvalue(dimes)))," dimes")
28   println(Int(round(getvalue(quarters)))," quarters")
```

The printed output is:

The Model to be Optimized:

Min 2.5 pennies + 5 nickels + 2.268 dimes + 5.67 quarters

Subject to

pennies + 5 nickels + 10 dimes + 25 quarters = 99
pennies ≥ 0, integer
nickels ≥ 0, integer
dimes ≥ 0, integer
quarters ≥ 0, integer

The Optimum Solution:

Minimum Weight = 31.546 grams
Achieved with:
4 pennies
0 nickels
7 dimes
1 quarters

Well, that's about it for this introduction to the Julia language. There is a lot more to learn and the best way to do that is to start using Julia to solve some problems.

The second best way is to refer to the docs:

https://julialang.org/

https://learnxinyminutes.com/docs/julia/

https://juliaobserver.com/packages